Hey there

THE LIFE OF EDMUND HOCKRIDGE

AS TOLD TO NEIL PATRICK

BLACKIE & CO PUBLISHERS LTD

A Blackie & Co Publishers paperback

© Copyright 2003
Neil Patrick

The right of Neil Patrick to be identified as the author of this work has been
asserted by him in accordance with the Copyright, Designs and Patents Act 1988

First published 2003

A CIP catalogue record for this title is available from the British Library
ISBN 1 84470 044 5

BLACKIE & CO PUBLISHERS LTD
107-111 Fleet Street
London EC4A 2AB

Edmund Hockridge (right) with author Neil Patrick

Edmund
Hockridge

Best wishes - Neil
Patrick

About the author

Neil Patrick has been a journalist for more than 40 years, and a music-lover since, as a child, he was struck by the joy his Granddad derived from listening to Handel's *Messiah* coming from the wireless.

While editing YOURS, the leading national magazine for older people, Neil interviewed Edmund Hockridge, who lived only a mile or so from the magazine offices. Edmund and his wife Jackie, who were at an age when most people are retired, were forging ahead with new plans, singing great songs, looking good and giving great pleasure to audiences throughout Britain. They epitomised the positive message the magazine tries to pass on to its readers.

The three became friends, and the magazine sponsored a series of Hockridge Family concerts nationwide (a bonus for Neil was that the sporting Hockridge sons, Murray and Stephen, were dragooned into playing in the village cricket team Neil captained!).

Hearing Edmund's stories of life in musicals, Neil was convinced that a biography should be written. For years, Edmund resisted the idea but finally relented and, with his wife Jackie, started the exhausting job of listing most of the appearances he made during a 50-year career, and drawing together recollections of some of the best – and worst! – moments.

What has emerged is a colourful and absorbing story, following Edmund's boyhood in Vancouver, his life down on the family farm, through service in wartime, and on to a half-century of delighting people with his singing and his company.

Many will also enjoy reading about the love that has underpinned Edmund's life as an entertainer – and to be reminded of the scores of great British stars he worked with in shows, concerts, cabarets, and on TV and radio. They will also savour the big moments in a long and distinguished career, and a glimpse into the private life he values so much.

* Neil Patrick continues to write columns in YOURS and, under the company name Now I Remember Ltd., is producing tapes and books giving a voice to the older generation.

Hey there

The bench scene in Carousel, with Laverne Burden. This was my audition piece.

CHAPTER
1

*"You know something
from Carousel?"*
"How about If I Loved You, sir?"

"OK. Whadd'ya know?"

The voice from deep in the darkened stalls of the theatre was gruff and impatient. It was understandable; auditions had been going on for three days and they seemed to be going nowhere. It now looked increasingly unlikely that in the assembled company of hopefuls – the big, the small, the long, the short and the tall – there was anyone around with all the right qualities for the part.

This was a lead role, and he would have to have stature and presence, to be "as tall and as strong as a tree" in fact, and have a baritone voice of power and sensitivity. And of course, the accent had to be right – American, or as near as dammit.

As Edmund Hockridge was called up, he replied with a courteous "Sir" – the curtness in the voice seemed to demand it. Although he was not especially hopeful, Edmund was thrilled just to be singing here; after all the Theatre Royal was one of the oldest and most famous theatres in the world.

Certainly a chance like this – coming out of the blue – was a great surprise so soon after arriving in England. Maybe the decision to sell up and make that 10,000-mile trip was going to be justified.

It was Autumn, 1950, and the producers of Carousel, recently arrived from Broadway, were having to find a new leading man as the American star, Stephen Douglas, had come to the end of his six-month work permit. So the hunt was on to find someone to step into the shoes – and the rather fetching tartan trews – of the male lead character, Billy Bigelow.

One morning Edmund received a phone call, and suddenly he was up there, on the Theatre Royal's massive stage, with that brusque voice challenging him to prove he was big enough in every way to be the new Billy.

§ § §

Edmund tells the story…

"The man on the phone was Teddy Holmes of Chappells Music in Bond Street. I knew that they controlled the British rights of Rodgers and Hammerstein musicals. Teddy's call was to ask whether I knew anything about Carousel.

CHAPTER ONE

When I said that I'd learned the music and that I thought the show was fabulous, he told me: 'Well, get yourself down to the Theatre Royal, Drury Lane.'

"In fact I'd seen Carousel in New York, with John Raitt in the lead, and sung some of the songs on my radio show in Canada. It was a wonderful musical and amazingly, in the light of what was to happen, I had the score with me when I was on the ship coming over to England.

"Carousel was playing there after its New York run, and he explained that the New York cast would not be getting work permits to carry on with the run in Britain. He said the producers were auditioning like mad to find a singer for the lead male role because Stephen Douglas would also be going back to the States.

What he said next filled me with hopeful anticipation. "You look a lot like John Raitt, your Canadian accent sounds American and, best of all, you don't have to have a work permit!" I had nothing to lose.

"What a thrill it was to enter the stage door of one of the world's most historic theatres, the place where the great David Garrick acted! Inside I found scores of hopefuls waiting to audition. There was every shape, size, age, accent and a wide range of nationalities. But because Carousel was fairly new in Britain, hardly anyone knew the songs.

"Someone called out my name and I stepped out onto a massive stage in front of a huge auditorium, which was like a vast, dark cave in front of me. The theatre has around 2,300 seats and from one of them, somewhere out there in the blackness, a voice growled 'OK. Whadd'ya know?'

" 'Something from Carousel, sir?' I replied. I automatically said 'sir' because the timbre of his voice and autocratic manner reminded me of some of the Canadian Air Force flight sergeants I'd met! "You know something from Carousel?" The voice was gruff and slightly incredulous. "Yes, sir. How about *If I Loved You*, sir?"

"In the corner of the stage sat a musician who later became a friend. It was Roy Lowe, brother of the theatre's orchestral conductor, and he was slouching in front of the upright piano; the boredom he was enduring, having played for three days of auditioning, was obvious. I asked him if he could transpose the song up half a tone to D flat. Many weeks later he told me laughingly that my request had come like manna from heaven (he recalled that he had thought: 'My God, here's someone who knows what key he wants to sing in!')

"I sang what is a beautiful proclamation of love, trying to express the full feeling of Hammerstein's gorgeous lyrics. The last note died away and the voice from the dark shouted; 'What else do you know from Carousel?'

"'The *Soliloquy*, sir' I replied. This seemed to take him by surprise, understandably because the Soliloquy lasts seven minutes and is a test for voice, memory and acting ability. I was allowed to have a go and did my best to recall how John Raitt in New York had walked onto the stage and poured forth the emotions Billy Bigelow felt on discovering that he was about to become a father, first wondering whether it would be a boy and, if so, how he would make a man of him, and then musing on the possibility that it would be a girl. If that happened, he vowed, he would do anything for her, even if it meant 'going out to make it, steal it, or take it, or die'.

"The voice in the dark, very interested now, asked whether I had done any musicals and I hurriedly replied, 'Oh yes, and five operas, and nine Gilbert and Sullivans'. I spoke quickly in the hope that he might not ask me what musicals I'd actually done, because I'd never done one! I felt at the time: 'Is this really happening to me?' But there was little time to think, because I found myself being told to go home to study a scene from the first act, which included the duet *If I Loved You* and involving Billy the fairground barker and Julie Jordan, the main female character, in their first romantic confrontation.

"I was up most of the night and arrived at the theatre at 10 am to meet the New York leading lady, Laverne Burdon. It was as if a dream was unfolding in front of me. We went through the entire scene, with me striving to control my nerves, and Laverne brilliantly holding the whole thing together. It went well and it began to sink in finally that my life was about to change.

"Musicals seemed to be right for the times – they were just what was needed to brighten things up in the aftermath of the war, and to my advantage, for once, baritones rather than tenors were taking star roles.

CHAPTER 2

"I wondered if I was an afterthought... or a failed attempt at a daughter!"

Edmund 'Ted' Hockridge left Vancouver for Britain for the second time when he was 31. Yet still, 50 years later, he would sometimes refer to it as 'his city' with an affectionate possessiveness that might suggest he still lived there. Over that half a century he had watched Vancouver develop into a fashionable, stylish and 'cool' 21st-century city. But the Vancouver he knew, and which lives on in memory, is far different. The place and his life are intermingled in a special way, in fact for a time the young city and youthful Ted grew up together.

Having seen much of the world, looking back he says there is no place he would rather have found himself as a boy. Vancouver was a city that was spreading outward and upward, as it became more and more prosperous. Ted was a boy growing tall and strong from sport and fresh air, learning from teachers he admired and brothers he adored, forging friendships, and learning about the harder side of life, all within the framework of a happy family life.

Vancouver was a paradise for the young and adventurous, a city with wilderness on the doorstep. It is surrounded by spectacular scenery on a breathtaking scale, with mountains, woods and inlets and fjord-like escarpments. Ted drank his fill of the pleasures that Nature had bestowed on his birthplace. "I loved my city boyhood years, everything about it," he says. "I simply revelled in being part of such a young, vibrant and beautiful place."

It was Vancouver's growing reputation as a city with the huge potential that lured his parents, Charles and Luella Hockridge, from their home in Ontario, where they had met and married in their home town of Cedarville, a few miles west of Toronto – on Christmas Day 1901, when Charles was 25 and Luella 22. They were third-generation Canadians, a mix of Devonshire and Yorkshire and with a splash of Scots in there somewhere. The northerly, Morayshire roots were entangled with the clan Murray, a name that was given to Ted's eldest brother and later to one of Ted's own sons.

His own father Charles was an athletic, bright and energetic character who enjoyed pitching a ball and hauling a rope for the town's tug-o'-war team as much as he loved to sing in choirs and barbershop groups. Luella was an apprentice-trained ladies' tailor and an excellent seamstress.

Although Charles had been brought up on the land, he spotted, and exploited, a business opportunity in Ontario, setting himself up with a general store. It was not as comfortable a job as it might sound. Charles would regularly have to make a 24-mile round trip to the railway station to collect goods to sell, with a horse and wagon in summer and with horse and sled in the bitter, snow-bound winters. His skill with horses led him to extend into horse-trading, in barns behind the store.

Suddenly they felt 'the call of the West'. In the Spring of 1913 they sold up and moved 3,000 miles from Ontario to the Pacific, with their three sons taking a seemingly endless rail journey (in fact it took four days). The trek was spectacular but also, we can guess, claustrophobic, the family being cloistered together with other families as the locomotive steamed its way through the plains and mountains.

Excitement must have grown as the train hit the wild and wonderful 650-mile stretch of line which had been blasted through the Rockies in the 1860s, and which formed the last leg of the journey. This stunningly spectacular section of the rail route across Canada is also an engineering masterpiece. Up to 5,000 men at a time were employed in blowing a path into seemingly immovable mountains that had effectively been a massive wall cutting off Vancouver from the rest of Canada.

The establishment of a rail link had been the making of Vancouver which was soon to be given another boost. Just as the Hockridges began to settle in, the Panama Canal opened and the city began to capitalise on its ability to ship goods to many corners of the world more competitively than before. The optimism generated by the economic factors favouring Vancouver's future compensated the city, perhaps, for what had been a tragic and spectacular false start when, on the (unlucky) thirteenth of June, 1886 – just two years after its incorporation as a city – Vancouver vanished in an afternoon!

A contemporary press cutting tells the story with brevity that is out of all proportion to the gravity of the incident…

VANCOUVER – A freak squall blew the flames from a forest clearing fire onto a shed this Sunday afternoon, and in a few hours Vancouver had disappeared. Buildings just vanished in a sheet of flame. Whole families, with their pets, ran into the water of False Creek. Others managed to escape along the Canadian Pacific Railway embankment or down Westminster Road. Virtually every building in the mostly wooden village of huts and cabins was destroyed and at least 50 people were reported killed trying to get into blazing buildings to save other people or treasured belongings.

§ § §

On arrival in the rebuilt Vancouver, the Hockridge family settled into a rented house and Charles found a job in the postal service. Soon he was able to set himself up in business with his first general store, at 16th Avenue and Heather. Within five years of arriving, using his considerable carpentry skills to good effect, he had helped to build a three-storey timber house at 910, 19th Avenue West. Pavements – or sidewalks – were not a priority, and when Ted was born there on August 9, 1919, planking edged the roads over the mud. In rural areas Model T Fords bounced along on 'roads' scattered with planks laid crossways to prevent the cars becoming stuck in the mud.

Ted had an extremely happy childhood. A joke he once made about his birth date reveals the openness of the relationships within the family, intimacy which was the exception rather than the rule in those stricter times, when children knew their place, and when there was an unspoken understanding that certain topics were no-go areas.

"I was born two days short of nine months after Armistice Day and of course there was quite a gap after the arrival of my youngest brother Jack. I wondered whether I was an afterthought, an 'accident', or a failed attempt for a daughter – I know they had the name Edwina ready, maybe hopefully! Although in those days youngsters did not have TV, access to explicit films or any form of porn, you still learned about sex. Thinking about my birthdates one day, after a history lesson, I came home from school, rushed into the house, and teased my darling mother about my calculations – and my theory: That I was nothing more than the product of excitement of my parents on learning that the war was over!

"Of course, she was a church-goer and a church organist and she went red in the cheeks and dashed out of the room. But she was wonderful about it. When Dad came home from work I heard her killing herself with laughter telling him what I'd said. You can't buy that sort of humour in a family."

Ted, born seven years after the last of three sons – Murray, Ralph (nicknamed Brick because of his red hair) and Jack – was given three kingly names, Edmund James Arthur and, as the 'baby' of the family, the three doting older brothers treated him royally, though they called him Ted. It was only later in life that Ted reverted to Edmund, when he needed to distinguish himself from a string of other entertainers who were called Ted – Ted Ray and Ted Andrews (Julie's father) among them.

Ted felt blessed by the affectionate protectiveness of his brothers all his life. He recalls: "Because I came into the world so much later than them, it was as if I was an only child but with the advantage of big brothers as role models. From each I gained something, knowledge or a skill or advice."

When he slipped (which he often did quite literally when learning to ice skate!) or if he faltered, there was a brotherly arm hauling him up and setting him right. His debt to them – and admiration for each of them – is encapsulated in a poignant line in a letter Ted wrote to his elderly brother Murray in the mid-1990s. It is all the more touching because it voices feelings that had lasted 70 years or more and it was written not long before Murray died… "You were very good to your kid brother…very generous and protective; firm, yes, but always a pal and teaching me useful things whenever we were together."

How proud Ted was when Brick became a Mountie, especially when Nelson Eddy and Jeanette Macdonald were shooting Rose Marie up in the Rocky Mountains and Brick was one of the Mounties the film-makers 'borrowed'. Ted was taken with a school party to watch the shooting from a distance and still remembers how special he felt that his brother was involved in such an exciting event.

Ted's earliest memory was being taken up to the roof garden on the 20th floor of the new Vancouver Hotel and being held in his father's arms so that he could see the magnificent mountain peaks called The Lions that looked down on the city. The magnificent scenery intruded into even the suburban areas of Vancouver where, with the gorgeous coastal mountain range on the skyline, there was always a sense of living in a rugged landscape. In the district where the Hockridge family lived, on the southern side of the city, there were Douglas firs 150ft high. When they were felled, as development spread, brushwood would spring up until, finally, builders won the battle against Nature by erecting houses.

Ted's first experience of getting close to the earth was in his own back yard. The soil that had sustained huge trees was very fertile and Luella put her strong creative talents to work, growing dahlias, gladioli, sweet peas and roses to enter in the annual flower show, and cultivating vegetables, raspberries and loganberries. Hens, cats, and dogs gave Ted first hand experience of animals, a passion that would last a lifetime.

Of special – and illicit – interest for playing were the Chinese Gardens. When he was four or five he and his chums would sneak into this area which had been laid out on land allocated to Chinese who had originally been brought to Canada to work on rail track-laying in the mountains. They had settled and set up their laundries, restaurants and vegetable gardens, in the same way that Seattle, Los Angeles, San Francisco, and many other cities, evolved 'Chinatowns'. The big attraction for Ted and his friends was that the gardens contained ponds – and ponds contain frogs, and fish!

Eventually the area was reclaimed by the city council and the gardens were transformed into six rugby pitches with a sports hall in the middle, a development that was to allow Ted to follow his other brothers into a range of sports. As the population was mostly British, rugby union was played at all the schools along with baseball, American football, ice hockey and lacrosse. Soccer had yet to take off.

At four, Ted had his first experience of 'school', a kindergarten, and of girls. There were none at home after all, and so understandably they aroused considerable curiosity. In fact, it was not long before he walked one of them home. She was the daughter of a neighbour and, reaching her home, he gave her a kiss. Unfortunately, the door was slightly ajar and the mother, looking on from inside, burst out laughing. Blushing furiously, the young Lothario scampered into his own home. He can still feel that flush of embarrassment!

Ted had loved school as much as he loved being out of it, exploring the mountains around him and the wild and watery places with names that were redolent of the days when explorers and settlers came, saw and named them… Grouse Mountain, Lost Lagoon, Howe Sound, Keats Island, Capilano Canyon.

He followed in the footsteps of his three older brothers, enrolling at Edith Cavell Public School. By this time, Murray was in his early years of study at the University of British Colombia; Brick and Ralph were in secondary school. Ted loved Cavell, where the headmaster was 'Papa' Gray, a man with great insight and understanding of young people, someone who balanced the need for sound education with sporting prowess. Ted recalls that he also had a wicked sense of humour…

"One winters' day I threw a snowball at a girl who'd been causing trouble in class. My missile, which was supposed to hit the girl as she stood on her doorstep, missed her, unfortunately, and splodged straight into the face of her mother as she opened the door." Next day, Ted found himself in Papa Gray's office, where he was told to hold out his hand. Ted obeyed, and six times the cane swished down, but each time missed his hand. Papa Gray said: "Don't breathe a word about this. The mother's a trouble maker, too – and I don't like them either."

His teachers had been brought over from Britain, and Ted got on well with all of them. One, a Scottish master called Mr Henderson, taught English grammar and literature and opened the door to a lifetime of enjoyable reading for Ted, starting with Ivanhoe, Treasure Island and A Tale of Two Cities. Mr Henderson had innovative ideas to stimulate interest in his subject. One day he said that he would allow the class to study John Masefield's poem Sea Fever for a few minutes. He announced that the first pupil to stand up and recite it from memory could have the rest of the afternoon off to spend in the library. The song version had always been a favourite of Ted's mother, and he had heard it many times… so guess who won?

Mr Henderson had been through the Battle of the Somme and described to his pupils some of his horrific experiences in the trenches. Ted and his friends were mesmerised and remember him expressing the hope that such a war should never happen again. Ironically, the world was already shaping up for a Second World War and when Ted was about to join the Royal Canadian Air Force, just after the war started, he met Mr Henderson on a bus. The teacher was philosophical but sad. "Here we go again!" he said. "Mankind never learns – but may you have luck on your side, son."

Mr Henderson's enthusiasm for sporting challenges led him to offer parents of some children, including Ted, to climb Grouse Mountain, on the North shore of Vancouver harbour, where he would teach them to ski. Ted's parents agreed and the party set off on the North Vancouver ferry in the early hours of the morning and then on a tramline that took them up the first thousand feet to Mosquito Creek.

The boys then climbed the remaining 3,000 feet up a rock-strewn trail littered with fallen trees, through forest and finally onto the plateau. There they were able to hire skis from a rugged character in a log cabin. After a happy day learning how to ski, they returned down the mountain in the dark following instructions to make lots of noise to deter bears and puma that frequented the area. They had no torches, relying on candles set in syrup tins. Ted will never forget the thrill of that expedition, or of a string of pleasurable experiences which could be summoned up by the mention of one word: Granthams.

This spot, really Granthams Landing, which lay in Howe Sound, was paradise for Ted and his brothers and they spent several unforgettable summer holidays in a landscape that resembled Scandinavian fjords. It was there that Murray helped Ted improve his swimming strokes to the point where he was chosen to swim for the school, and it was there that he learned how to sail, catch salmon and dress them. He also looked on and learned as Murray, an excellent carpenter as his father was, built a superb summer cottage. An extra bonus of the site was that the boys could see whales and porpoises close up.

In a letter to Murray, late in his older brother's life, Ted recreated the idyllic experiences they had shared. He wrote: "Granthams! It sparks the loveliest memories imaginable. What wonderful days we had up there! Remember the first sail boat you guys built together and salmon fishing out through the gap? Remember how I was stung by a swarm of hornets and had to dash down an outcrop two or three hundred feet high to plunge myself into the muddy stream? Man, did they sting! I also recall the huge swing you put up in the trees in front of your cabin, and the Union steam ships that went by."

§ § §

Ted's reminiscences of idyllic long-ago summers are countered by some instances of the harder aspects of real life intruding. He was growing up fast and, in doing so, was encountering tragedy for the first time.

First there was the shocking death of a young man who helped Ted's father in his business. Seymour Woodall had taught Ted the intricacies of baseball pitching. The family was devastated when he became ill with meningitis and died. Even more traumatic was the drowning of a youngster he knew. The boy had gone with others to swim near Twin Islands, a sheltered area of water that was a haven for huge booms of floating logs, which were pulled by teams of tugs to the sawmills. Like other boys, he found it great fun to dive off the logs but being a bit of a daredevil he risked a dive under the logs but lost his way, could find no way to surface and failed to reappear. Ted was also saddened by the news that the son of a neighbour had been arrested for bank robbery, and then appalled when his sister killed herself out of a sense of shame.

Ted's liking for girls and admiration for their beauty had been aroused long ago, when he cast his eyes over the girls of his age in his school (where, incidentally, Yvonne de Carlo, later to be a Hollywood star, was a pupil). In church, his mind was usually more on the young ladies than on higher matters. But his innocent awakening to the appeal of the opposite sex was unsettled by an incident that shocked him and angered his family.

Ted was delivering groceries when a young woman, provocatively dressed and holding a glass of wine, came to the door and showed more interest in him than in her food order. Not an easy situation to deal with when you are just 12. As a youngster with an incomplete understanding of sex, he was also disturbed to hear of a girl from school who had been molested by her father, who was later jailed, and of how two of Murray's friends at university were having to have a 'shotgun wedding'. In his mind Ted conjured up a picture of the young groom being led to the altar at gunpoint, like a sacrificial lamb!

But every glimpse he had of the darker side of life was countered by many pleasures and happy times. One special moment came when he had to make a delivery to the Shaughnessy Heights area of Vancouver where the city's elite had their homes. There, one Christmas, after he had climbed the 49 steps to the impressive residence of the Lieutenant Governor of British Colombia, the butler handed him a five dollar tip as a reward for his reliable delivery of newspapers, making him, temporarily, one of the rich kids of the city.

In the background of his life was music, music – and more music. From an early age his parents, great music lovers, took him to listen to choir concerts and to symphony concerts, to the ballet, to visiting opera companies, and to hear oratorios. Having a mother who was a pianist helped greatly with his early musical education, and encouraged him to learn the piano. He never excelled at playing, despite the best efforts of his teacher, Miss Pritchard. (Ted recalls that she was very religious and jokes that this was obvious when, hearing him play, she would always say: "My God, My God!"). But the learning of musical theory was to prove invaluable later in life, enabling Ted to read music rapidly when he began to sing professionally, and to talk the same language as conductors and accompanists.

§ § §

Barn raising at the farm of my grandfather, John Hockridge, at Cedarville, Ontario. Although he is difficult to make out my father, Charles, is circled in the picture. All beams, braces, struts and rafters were measured and shaped in advance and then locked together in just a few hours using hardwood pegs.

A family group – from the left Murray, Jack, my dad Charles, my mum Luella, with me in front and brother Ralph (Brick) alongside.

Me as an 11-year-old (known as 'Teddy') taking my darling mum for a canoe ride

Me (right) as a 17-year-old with dad and my brothers. From the left, Murray, a headmaster, Ralph, a Mountie, and Jack who was an industrialist.

CHAPTER

3

Taking the seven-foot saw, Ted
and Dad would work in harmony
until a big slice of wood fell away

Charles Hockridge's business survived the stock market crash of 1929 but he had to sell his few acres of land, in an area called Burnaby, to cushion himself from the financial collapse that was ruining thousands. Ironically, had he been able to hang on to the land for a few years he would have been a millionaire. Sale of the land, which was eventually in demand for factory and warehouses, plus the timber on it, would have ensured a financially secure future for the family. As it was, Charles became unwell as the new decade dawned and began to pine for life on the land, a return to the fresh air and physical work he had known in boyhood. In 1933, he sold his two stores and bought a farm 40 miles away up in the Fraser Valley.

Ted had just started school at King Edward High in the city. The move would mean that he would have to enrol at a new school – Cloverdale High – and catch a school bus at 8 am for the 20-mile journey every day. But any anxiety he might have felt about the big move for the family was soon calmed by the realisation that here was a new adventure, with new skills to be learned, and with the added excitement of being able to care for animals.

Dad sensibly prepared his boy, now a tough 14-year-old with energy to spare, for the new life by arranging for him to go to the farm of a friend he had known back in Ontario, to learn how to milk cows, groom animals, and cut hay. There were three older boys in the family to show him the way. The crash course in animal husbandry enabled Ted to be of immediate help when his father bought in the cattle, together with the pigs and hens – up to 1,000 of them – which, along with the orchard and the garden, would make the Hockridges fairly self-sufficient, as well as creating a living.

Ted loved the changing of the seasons, felt much more keenly in the country than in the city. He has fond memories of walking among the 60 trees in the orchard and selecting a type of apple called Northern Spy, the taste of which has stayed with him, although he has never come across the variety since. Home-baked bread, clover honey, hearty breakfasts and cups of cocoa, to drive out the biting cold of the winters in the Valley, also live on as comforting memories of happy but physically demanding times.

24

CHAPTER THREE

When two hands were not enough and four were needed, Ted was there. Taking the seven-foot saw to tackle a fallen tree with a girth equal to the height of a man, Ted and Dad would take a side each and, moving in harmony, yet hidden from each other by the timber bulk, see-saw away until a huge slice of wood fell, to supply fuel to get them through the bitter winters.

The Hockridges had electricity but no running water. There was a well outside, and this provided all they needed except, sometimes, in the height of summer, when it would run low. Although the well was a daunting 28ft deep, the only answer was to go down there and dig it deeper, bucketing up the soil from the bottom. This they did successfully one summer but a family living nearby suffered a terrible tragedy doing the same thing. There were three boys and the eldest went down their well first. He did not reply when the other called to him so another followed, and when he did not reply, the third sent for help. Methane gas had fatally overcome both boys.

Ted was also affected by a freak accident involving the boy of another neighbour. It was common to use explosives to uproot the stumps of felled trees and when this was being done on land not far from the Hockridges' farm, the fuse failed and the stump and explosive was left. The father warned his son to stay away from it but some time later the fuse reignited and the explosion killed the boy. Ted had been given a chilling lesson in how dangerous life could be – especially where individuals, sometimes in isolated areas, were confronted with problems they knew they had to resolve themselves.

One day a student teacher joined the Hockridges as a boarder, and as this young man had a car, he and Ted decided to motor up Fraser Canyon to a spectacular waterfall they had heard about. There, they found a tributary to the Fraser River and decided to climb up the mountain tracking its course to the waterfall near the top. Lying across the top of this waterfall was a huge, fallen pine tree, spanning a breathtaking drop of a couple of hundred feet. The boys decided that it would be fun to shin across it.

Fearlessly, they worked their way along the four-foot thick trunk and then carefully worked their way back. Ted thought nothing more about this but some time later he retraced his steps to the waterfall, looked up and saw that the tree had split and fallen into the chasm. It made him shudder, and think: "Wow! That could have been the end of me!"

Ted's life was physically testing. The day started at 5. 30 am and he worked around the farm until 7. 30. By this time his mother had prepared a bacon-and-eggs breakfast for the ravenous Hockridge Junior to devour before the school bus arrived. It was a demanding routine. Ted remembers that sometimes there was a temptation to drop off to sleep during the duller lessons but even when he could rest, at lunchtime, there was always baseball or other sports to be played, and suddenly, somehow, the tiredness disappeared.

He was at that age when the body's batteries never seem to need recharging. The physical life, lived in beautiful surroundings, suited him perfectly and shaped him not only in terms of physique, but in other ways, for the life he was destined to lead. After all, what better for a singer, in an age when they were expected to fill theatres with sound without the help of microphones, than to be lifting, carrying, sawing and chopping in the pristine air of a mountainside? And what better preparation for roles that called for imposing physique? Come to think of it, what better for a vet of the future – a real possibility in Ted's mind as a 'proper" career – than to be surrounded by animals to care for?

The idea of being a vet, or a surgeon, grew stronger as he grew older. There is no room on farms for sentimentality about animals but Ted's dedication amounted to more than the simple call of duty; he found himself identifying strongly with animals that were suffering.

He believes that his tender protectiveness of animals dates back to an incident when he was a small child. He was four, and staying at an uncle's farm on the prairies for a summer. One day he wandered in to a barn and came across an appalling scene. A cow had been strung up by the legs for slaughter and as it bellowed in fear an axe was swung at its throat. That was the reality of farming – animals were bred to be eaten, as well as providing milk but it was a fact of life learned too early. Ted recalls: "It was then I think that I must have decided that I'd much rather save an animal than kill it."

Years later, two incidents, concerning humble hens, illustrate a humanitarian instinct that led Ted to feel that he would end up tending either animals or human beings.

A Leghorn cockerel used for breeding had become ill and Ted, now quite knowledgeable from close contact with animals, noticed that its wattles and comb were an unhealthy colour. Normally a sick bird would have had its neck wrung and be thrown into the boiler for pig feed but Ted found this solution difficult to live with. He suspected that there was a blockage in the crop, so, finding a razor blade and cotton and thread, he slit open the crop, cleared it of a piece of wood that the bird had accidentally eaten, and, having washed the area with carbolic soap, he then sewed up the wound. The cockerel survived to crow another day.

§ § §

Towards the end of his career, Ted wrote an article for the Edmund Hockridge Appreciation Society magazine in which he described, graphically, life on the farm and how, appalled by the seeming callousness of Nature, he intervened to save another bird that had no economic value. He described this, with humour, as his first love affair, although as it turned out the love was all on one side – the chicken's!

He wrote: "A country boy's day meant being up before dawn, and the first thing you did was encase yourself in ice-cold togs, plunge into the darkness and switch the lights on in the stables, hatcheries and buildings housing our thousand laying hens. The next two hours I spent shoulder-to-shoulder with Dad trying to beat the clock. There was ice to break to enable us to pump drinking water, there were troughs to fill with feed, perches to clear, and fresh bedding to spread. Then we would have to milk the cows to milk and feed the pigs.

"Our loyal helper throughout was Tiny, our little terrier. After I'd enjoyed a huge farm breakfast, she would bark me off on to the school bus as it slithered to a stop outside our gate. By the way, the bus often had difficulty in snow, and we kids were often asked to get out and push; of course, being kids sometimes we mischievously contrived to slide the bus into the roadside ditch to try to win a day off!"

Ted then described how, one morning when he was looking over a couple of hundred newly-hatched chicks under a large electric brooder, he noticed a chick that was isolated and bleeding from wounds. She looked disorientated and when he scooped her up he noticed her head weaving back and forth. He suddenly realised that she was blind and, as such, doomed. He placed a snug box near the kitchen stove, fed her with milk for a time and then, over the following weeks, weaned her on to a mash of chick food. She grew steadily, developed snow-white plumage, and healthy bright-red wattles… and the idea that Ted was her mother!

"Eerily for me," Ted said in his article, written for his fans, "her main interest in life was the sound of my voice; it was her compass guide, helping her locate herself, and my whereabouts on the farm. Hearing me, she would cock her head daintily and then trot to me like a little puppy going to heel. Tiny, and Molly our cat, accepted her as just another pet. After a few months she proudly plopped down her first egg, the first of many. I was proud of my rescue operation and she thrived, for nine months, until I had to leave home for a temporary job in Vancouver. Dad looked after her when I left but when I had gone she refused to eat. Dad wrote to me to tell me the news that she had just faded away through lack of food. Funny, but I can still feel choked at the reliance that this little creature had on me."

At 16, Ted, the dispenser of tender loving care to helpless hens, was on the receiving end of dedicated care himself and he believes that it probably saved his life. He had started to feel ill and develop a high temperature and as his condition worsened it became clear he had contracted meningitis. For four days he lay in a semi-coma, with a temperature soaring to 104 degrees. His mother applied mustard plasters to the chest and hot compresses to his forehead, urging him through what was a life-or-death crisis. It was touch and go for a while. He was left with two mementos of the drama – a blistered forehead from the hot compresses, and a lifelong tendency to occasional nosebleeds, a weakness that was to affect his role in the coming war.

§ § §

CHAPTER THREE

As Ted moved towards graduation from high school his career options seemed to be singing, or working as a vet, or even as a surgeon after university and training. He was – and remains – fascinated by medical science, and two of his long-standing friendships in later life were, significantly, with the pioneering surgeon who helped save his singing career, and the London osteopath who treated him for years.

Music had become central to his life, whether as a listener, or a singer. On Saturday afternoons he would follow broadcasts from the Metropolitan Opera Company in New York, absorbing a large repertoire of baritone roles along the way. At other times he would tune in to performances by Alan Jones or Lawrence Tibbet, or sing along with Bing Crosby or Nelson Eddy, and listen to symphony concerts. He sang in church choirs, in school choirs and in male voice choirs. Everywhere he went he sang, on the farm and in the forest. He had started to win prizes as a solo singer and there was a growing recognition that his voice was something quite special.

When Ted was around 18 his father took on a young helper and Ted was free to earn some money and take his first steps to independence. He moved into the city, and got a daytime job in a factory making laminated wooden skis for aircraft, so that he could take a night job as an usher at the Vancouver Auditorium. This entailed taking visitors and fans to the dressing rooms of the famous entertainers and musicians who performed there on tour, the idols he had heard over the airwaves. Suddenly he was within touching distance of superstars of the day – Paul Robeson, Jeanette Macdonald and Nelson Eddy, Gigli, Arthur Rubinstein. Ted was also absorbing the magical ambience of a major concert hall, the expectant thrill as the lights dimmed, the rustling of programmes, the first notes from the orchestra pit.

His dream was that one day he might be up there on the stage rather than out there, anonymous, in front of it as a spectator. He was given hope that this was not just a fanciful idea when he received approval and encouragement from an expert source, a famous singer. Realising that Ted's voice might indeed be as special as they thought it was, the matrons of a

Vancouver ladies' club arranged for John Charles Thomas, lead baritone with the New York Metropolitan Opera Company, to hear Ted sing.

He was taken to the Vancouver hotel where Thomas was staying while performing in the city during a tour, and was ushered into Thomas's suite where there was a piano and his accompanist. Thomas's recording of *The Blind Ploughman*, a classic ballad, was popular at the time, and when Ted was asked by the great man what he would like to sing, undaunted, he replied that he would like to sing that.

At the end of the song, Thomas said: "Very good. Now would you like to hear me sing it?" Ted listened, fascinated and thrilled. Finally, Thomas said: "You have a natural voice of quality. I think you could be a success but you must give priority to your education. Get into university and see where your singing takes you. Keep singing at all times. Who knows?" As it turned out, both furthering his singing and going to university were casualties of the outbreak of war.

Ted loved aircraft and, as war began to look inevitable, he began to foster hopes of becoming a pilot. He enjoyed making models of aircraft and flying them – in fact it was the mistreatment of one of his models that led Ted, normally a pacifist, into his first fight. One day, a boy who was renowned at school for bullying, picked up a big and impressive aircraft Ted had made and attempted to launch it. But rather than holding it well above his head, for a clear take-off, he held it by the nose – and as he thrust it forward the wing hit his head. To Ted's horror, the plane was damaged. This was a step too far, and, with hackles up, Ted waded in and took his anger out on the startled lout. For some time afterwards he basked in the admiration of his school friends.

When he finished secondary school, Ted matriculated, having excelled at maths, geography and English, and was now equipped to go to university. He began to take classes locally in college but as the war approached it was clear that military service was a likelier option than going to university, and of the three Services, the Royal Canadian Air Force was the clear choice.

Shortly before he signed up, Ted took his father to the new

Vancouver Airport where they saw, with excitement, the first Lockheed Electra to land in Canada.

He decided that in his last week before enlistment in the RCAF he would immerse himself in some music. A touring Italian opera company was performing La Traviata. Unfortunately the performance was not all it might have been. In fact Ted found himself intrigued because the tenor, who had magnificent arias to show off, had a heavy cold and rather than risk the high notes, kept dropping down an octave. He left the theatre pondering on the precariousness of the singing profession and later in life learned at first hand how frustrating it was for any singer to be afflicted with health problems that affected the voice.

Just before Ted left for initial training, brother Brick, whose unwavering support made the nick-name seem especially appropriate, did what older brothers were supposed to do for kid brothers setting out to explore the big wide world. He took him out, introduced him to drink, warned him about excess, and about the problems women could get you into.

Ted listened intently: After all Brick was a Mountie, a man who had seen a thing or two, and a brother to look up to.

§ § §

orporal (later commissioned)
ockridge of the R.C.A.F.
broadcast during the

During initial RCAF training in St Thomas, Ontario

Above: Corporal Hockridge broadcasting. Right: a local boy makes good!

GOLD MEDALIST — LA
Ted Hockridge (above), son
Mr. and Mrs. C. C. Hockridg
Newton, B. C., was award
the gold medal recently f
leading his class as an a
frame mechanic for the sixt
fourth entry, St. Thomas' Tec
nical Station, R.C.A.F. He a
tended King Edward Hig
School here and Surrey Hig
School, Cloverdale.

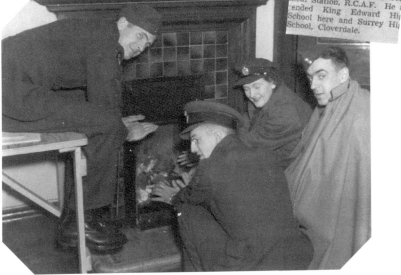

And we thought Canada was cold! Ted left, posted to London at the RCAF HQ in Lincolns Inn Fields, fights the British winter.

CHAPTER
4

"I would like you to become an instructor", said the CO. "No, sir", said Ted

"I beg your pardon," the CO replied

As for most young men, the outbreak of war presented Ted Hockridge with the prospect of adventure and a chance to travel. For many new recruits thoughts of the future were tinged with fear and uncertainty, and although Ted did wonder about the risks war entailed, he was not unduly worried. "I was ready for it; it was the right time, and my main emotion was a feeling of excitement," he says. For his father Charles it was different. Having four sons, quite naturally his pride in knowing they were serving their country was tempered with deep anxiety.

As he said goodbye, he clasped the outstretched hand of his youngest, soon-to-be AC Ted Hockridge of the RCAF. Charles was a product of his time, a time in which it was best to suppress feelings. Hugging between men, even between father and son, was an embarrassingly intimate thing to do, whatever the depth of love that lay locked inside. No such inhibitions affected Brick. Ted was to write later, "I wondered if I would get through the war intact, and as I left it was my big brother who was relaxed enough to give me something my father couldn't, even though we loved each other greatly. He could only shyly give me a hearty but obviously deeply-felt handshake. Brick's bearhug was something I've never forgotten and I ensure that I hug my own sons every day."

Brick's brotherly talk the night before was still fresh in Ted's mind as he stepped onto the train for Toronto. Three days later it pulled into sidings at the city exhibition centre, which was being used as barracks. In keeping with a long tradition, those who had completed training indulged in some mickey-taking as the rookies arrived and began being shaped for military life. After being fitted for a uniform, checked medically and given an injection – at the thought of which one big recruit keeled over! – there was parade practice and guard duty. Ted made an early good impression; while on guard he challenged an approaching figure and was amazed to learn that it was Billy Bishop, a former First World War flying ace who had become Air Marshal. The new recruit was rewarded for his vigilance with a leave pass.

After his initial training, Ted was posted to St Thomas, Ontario, near

Lake Erie, for a six-week course. Not only did he grow up there, visiting night clubs and learning what drink could do to a man, and seeing the seedier side of life, he excelled at his studies as an air frame mechanic and finished the course with top marks and a gold medal to show for it. News filtered back to Vancouver and the local paper reported on his success.

Still longing to fly, and hoping to apply for air crew, on a weekend pass he visited a nearby RCAF aerodrome and went up in an Avro Anson with an old school chum, now a pilot officer. Even in this slow-moving aircraft, as it was thrown into a few climbs and dives, a nose bleed, caused by the ever-changing air pressure, started and he was forced to acknowledge that his boyhood meningitis had probably made the problem permanent so far as flying was concerned. The absolute rules of flying were: No vision problems, no colour blindness and no nose bleeding. So early in the war, this quite possibly saved his life, as many Canadian pilots were to become casualties, including lots of his closest friends.

Instead, the CO at St Thomas interviewed him to discuss his future and told Ted he was to become an instructor, as Canadian instructors were having to be installed to enable British airmen to return to Britain. Ted had by this time hopes of going overseas, and his reply was a courteous but curt "No, sir," to which the CO replied, "I beg your pardon? You have just won a medal for your trade, and you are to become an instructor."

Ted was adamant, and the CO warned him in no uncertain terms that there would be 'consequences'. He would be posted overseas – which was just what Ted had been hoping for, especially as he would be going to Britain, a country he had a fondness for. Around him in Vancouver were lots of English migrants, his teachers had been Brits, he had played British sports and he loved his boys' annuals at Christmas, books that were full of material which was characteristically English.

§ § §

Ted left from the port of Halifax and there bumped into Alan Davidson, an old pal from school. They were to sail in a cruise liner, the Louis Pasteur, although the voyage to Greenock would turn out to be a far from tranquil cruise. In fact, the ship they were allocated to had been built to do service in the placid Mediterranean, and was far from equipped to ride out the worst weather the North Atlantic could come up with. Not only that, the Louis Pasteur was heavily laden, even top heavy. Cabins that would have been comfortable berths for a couple cruising in the Med were packed with ten or twelve servicemen stacked in bunks to accommodate the 5,000 she was carrying.

The Louis Pasteur sailed for Britain with two fast merchantmen and two destroyers. About two thirds into the voyage a big storm blew up and the ship began to roll heavily in the increasing waves. A concern was that with so many on board, the ship might keel over and so she was turned into wind and for 36 hours nose-dived and pitched into the huge waves, until the storm began to abate. Ted said: "Two of the six ships of our convoy disappeared in the storm and to this day I don't know what happened to them. What I do know was that our captain said we came within a couple of degrees of capsizing, before we turned into the wind." Ted had always been a sailor in Vancouver and was untroubled by the violent pitching, but many of the men suffered terrible sea sickness.

At one point in the voyage, Ted got a chance to sing for other airmen. The problem was that the only musical venue was the sergeant's mess – and Ted was then of the lowest rank. Alan Davidson, who was a sergeant, came up with the ideal solution: He loaned Ted one of his uniforms for his flying visit to the mess, where he delighted the company – and raised morale – with a few songs.

As the ship – full of young men going out into the world – approached the Scottish coast, they were given spiritual advice from the chaplain, and more down-to-earth guidance as to the perils facing the unwary. 'French safes' were handed out and there was much laughter as some of the cheekier lads launched inflated 'safes' over the chaplain's head.

Ted was transported south with others to the Royal Canadian Air Force reception centre established in Bournemouth. The Pavilion Theatre was the admin centre; the Winter Gardens had become the mess hall. He had no inkling then but a dozen years later Ted would see the Pavilion Theatre in a different light – from the stage as the male lead in Carousel as it went on tour from Drury Lane. There were several thousand young Canadians in Bournemouth at any one time (and the local girls loved the fact!). The airmen were split up into groups and were despatched to air bases all over Britain.

After ten days, Ted's unit set off by train up into Lincolnshire where they were dropped off at Louth, and, in ice-cold lorries, transported to North Coates Fittes, ten miles from Grimsby, an aerodrome with only a dyke between the runways and the North Sea. His new squadron was 407 Coastal Command, known as 'the Demon Squadron' for their sensational sinking of enemy ships off Holland, using low-level bombing. Ted's squad was housed in a shed-like building outside the aerodrome, and here he and his fellow Canadian airmen, surrounded by windswept flat lands, thought they might freeze to death. Although they were used to bitter but much drier Canadian winters, the penetrating damp chill of weather from over the North Sea seemed to get into their bones.

Lockheed Hudsons were arriving at the base from America regularly and there were raids on shipping nearly every night. Ted's work on maintaining the aircraft was cold, dirty and uncomfortable and it was a long trip into Grimsby for a hot shower or bath but he soon had his first taste of English hospitality, and a chance to thaw out in the warmth of a family atmosphere. An RAF pal invited him to his home in Sheffield, where Ted found the people welcoming and kindly, a trait which he believed was not influenced in the least by the fact that he had brought with him a thousand cigarettes and a parcel of food.

Ted has vivid memories of dramas during the frenzied activity of wartime operations. One day a top pilot, known for his flamboyant flying, overshot the runway and came within twenty yards of a torpedo dump. Not surprisingly, everyone dived for cover. There was a second aerodrome, some distance away, and one night a plane came in, overshot, pulled up prematurely, stalled and crashed. Although returning flights would normally shed their bombs before touching down, this aircraft had not released them and, as Ted watched in horror, there were explosions and several airmen were killed, including a boy Ted had gone to school with.

He watched, and wondered what would have happened to him had he been able to become a pilot. Swordfish biplanes, along with the Demon Squadron's Hudsons were sent up the French coast to tackle two German battleships – the Scharnhorst and the Gneisenau – attempting to slip up the Channel from Brest. Around half of them were shot out of the sky. Ted recalls one tall handsome American pilot who should never have been on this raid because he was injured. He was ordered to go, and Ted, with a feeling of premonition, felt at the time he was watching someone who knew he would not be coming back. He didn't.

The squadron had to be rebuilt, and was moved to Thorney Island on the South coast, not far from Portsmouth. There was a fear at the time that a German invasion was imminent, and one day everyone was called into a hangar where the CO addressed the men, saying that they were now effectively on the front line. They were ordered to dig trenches and install machine gun emplacements. Chillingly, the CO added – perhaps by way of encouragement! – that there were huge guns behind Arundel and they would be blasting the aerodrome off the map if it was clear the Germans were gaining a foothold. A comforting thought…

§ § §

One incident, above all others, brought home to Ted the part played by the fates in deciding who would be a casualty of war, and who would be spared to fight another day.

Ted describes how by fateful chance he dodged death…

"Our squadron was re-building with new planes and fresh crews, straight from training bases in Canada. The boys were being sent out on familiarisation flights around Britain, beginning with what we called 'box flights', a sort of circular tour which was in fact rectangular. On this particular day 'G for George' was being seen off on this sort of flight on a route that took the aircraft from the Portsmouth area, west to Torquay, north to Bristol, east to Outer London and then south again to Thorney Island. As always one or two more experienced squadron members went along for the ride to keep a general eye on things. And so we went off in Jeeps to the dispersal area, located 'George' and went through routine preparations for take off.

"The young pilot began taxiing along the runway but accidentally accelerated one engine too heavily and a wheel dropped off the edge of the runway into deep mud. Full power from both engines produced nothing; the starboard undercarriage was embedded in the mud, good and proper. A Jeep went back to the hangar for help and after a lot of tractor pulling, the lumbering bomber became unstuck.

"By the time 'George' had taxied to the control tower, more than 45 minutes had been lost. Final orders and charts were being exchanged, ready for take-off, when Flight Sergeant Evans suddenly appeared and shouted: 'Hockridge – don't go. I need you here!' And so I was called off. G for George finally took off and tragically was shot down by a roving German fighter over Lyme Bay. If the time spent righting the plane hadn't been lost, it might have had a perfectly uneventful flight. Certainly if I hadn't been called off the plane, I wouldn't be here today."

But as well as dramas, there were moments of light relief. When the squadron, with new crews and new planes, moved to Bircham Newton, near Sandringham, in Norfolk, one newly-arrived veteran pilot who, although a very experienced "bush pilot" from Northern Canada, had never flown a Hudson, took out and flew over the coast around Hunstanton. He swooped low over the fields and through the trees inland, obviously enjoying a pleasure trip. The CO ordered him to report in and asked whether he had been flying over the royal estate. He owned up and was told that there had been a phone call to say that as a result of the one-man aerial flypast the entire royal herd at Sandringham had stopped giving milk. Evidently, the royal household was not amused!

On another occasion, the aerodrome was closed down and the airmen were told to stay in their barracks. At dusk, a blue plane without markings touched down and re-fuelled and then took off. Ted later learned that this was the first Mosquito, being tested on a long flight to Norway and back. At the controls was Geoffrey de Havilland himself.

Ted was being sent down regularly to London by this time to sing for the BBC Forces Broadcasts. During leave from his base near Grimsby he had visited the Beaver Club – the Canadian forces' club in Trafalgar Square – and had been fooling around singing. After he'd given an off-the-cuff rendition of *Rose Marie* to a piano accompaniment, a civilian approached him and said: "Excuse me, son, but I'm from the BBC and I'd like to take you along to Piccadilly to meet the people I work with."

Ted obliged and they went into a cinema that had been converted into a BBC studio. There, one of the nation's leading bands, under Jack Payne, and a young girl singer called Anne Shelton, had just finished recording and Ted was introduced to them. Ted's escort announced: "We could use this boy – he's got a nice voice." He then asked Ted to sing again, and approval was instant.

The Beaver Club soon became a launch pad for Ted's talents, and some time after another visit, the Hockridge family back in Vancouver were able to read with pride a news item in the local newspaper. Beneath a picture of Ted and a headline *SINGS FOR DUCHESS* it described how a local boy, now an LAC in England, had made good in Britain by "charming the Duchess of Kent with his singing at the second anniversary party of the Beaver Club." The report ended: "He sang, in a rich baritone voice, *Carry Me Back To The Lone Prairie…* and a swing band, composed of airmen and soldiers also entertained, the Duchess joining in singing *Pack Up Your Troubles.*"

Ted was becoming as much a singer as he was an airman, a point that was brought home to his CO by more requests that Ted be 'posted' for 24 hours to the BBC. Permission was granted with a proviso that it 'must not happen too often.' By the middle of the war Ted – now Corporal Hockridge – had sung on radio with great orchestras and bands of the day and the Air Force decided that his talents could be best used in PR work at the five-storey HQ in Lincoln's Inn Fields. By a strange quirk of fate, 50 years later, Ted's eldest son Ian would work in the very same building, as head of advertising for a media company.

§ § §

CHAPTER FOUR

Ted was cautious about forming relationships with women, and kept in mind the prevailing warnings about the dangers of VD, and of mixing with 'the rough stuff'. He heeded advice that it was best to wait to find a 'nice girl' and that is just what happened, although Ted feels that the girl he was about to meet, a tiny Wren called Eileen Elliott, had been steered his way by well-meaning comrades and BBC producers.

Eileen, just five foot tall, worked in Lord Mountbatten's office. She was the daughter of hoteliers in the Isle of Wight and was a pleasant and likeable companion, and after they had spent a couple of leaves together she suggested marriage. Ted felt he was too young, and anyway, they had only known each other for a short time. But then, there was a war on, and everyone was conscious of the fact that life might be very short indeed. As Ted says: "I was young and rather naïve but she was a nice person and an attractive little lady and we finally decided to get married, although I can still clearly recall that at the time I felt a slight sense of unease about such a commitment."

The wedding was on the Isle of Wight and Ted recalls sitting on the cliff-top lawn of the Sandown hotel run by Eileen's parents and seeing three planes coming towards them almost at sea level. They roared up to 50 feet above the young newlyweds, with the swastikas clearly visible as they zoomed towards their target, the radar station on Ventnor Hill.

Ted was singing more and more on forces' broadcasts and caught the ear of a fellow Canadian, Sandy Macpherson, best known as an organist but then producing shows in wartime Britain. In an internal BBC memo, Sandy moved from the subject of the note – "A crooning troubadour" who was hoping for a place in a show – to another singer he had heard of, "Ted Hockeridge – I am not sure about the spelling," he wrote. He then asks whether this singer's services could be obtained: "I heard him in one or two Canadian Forces broadcasts and he seemed to have a remarkably good voice." The memo said. "If you know anything about him… I should be more than grateful."

Ted was by now Sgt. Ted Hockridge, working in public relations, radio and photography and, outside his job, becoming something of a cult figure with his BBC Forces broadcasts. He was moved out to work from

Bentley Priory, near Bushey, and here his singing experience was widened when he met George Baker, lead baritone of the D'Oyly Carte Opera Company. He was thrilled to be given lessons in the Gilbert and Sullivan patter roles. Ted, and Eileen, who was now pregnant, were living in a rented house in Bushey and after their son, Ian, was born, it was George who loaned Ted money to help the couple buy their own house in the same area.

Some time after moving in, the couple had a frightening experience. While Ian lay in his pram under trees at the bottom of the garden Ted spotted a V1 flying bomb coming over the hill from the Stanmore direction. Suddenly the motor cut out and it plunged straight towards them. He told Eileen to get into the Anderson shelter while he ran to the pram and struggled to release Ian from his restraining straps, then dashed into the house, before diving to safety. They emerged to find that bombs had taken the roofs off several houses nearby and had left a fifty-foot-wide crater in an adjacent field, leaving the dead bodies of several tethered goats strewn around the ground.

By the time D-Day was being planned, Ted – by then posted to Ford Aerodrome, near Arundel – had behind him an impressive list of appearances on radio shows including the popular Johnny Canuck's Review and, although at the time he regarded his singing merely of a pleasant sideline to his RCAF work, his name was becoming more and more well-known to the British public.

Suddenly, two days before D-Day, when he was standing by to go over on D-Day Plus 3, he was ordered to go to London. He was told to go to the Langham Hotel opposite Broadcasting House, and to find Room 22 on the second floor. There he encountered a group of young men in uniform, all of whom had experience of broadcasting or other entertainment. Cecil Madden, Head of Light Entertainment for the BBC was there along with Colonel David Niven.

"Gentlemen," said Madden, "we are about to set up what will be called the Allied Expeditionary Forces Network of the BBC. Its purpose will be to support our forces and keep up morale as of the landing. All of you have experience of some kind in radio production. We have arranged with your commanding officers that you should be seconded to the BBC as our production staff; you will be literally, civilians in uniform."

Ted listened, intrigued. He was one of the few in the room who knew that D-Day was the day after tomorrow. Madden continued: "You will work mostly in Broadcasting House where you will have access to military entertainment units including the British band of the Allied Expeditionary Force, under George Melachrino, the Canadian Band of the AEF under Captain Robert Farnon, and joining us soon, the American Band under Captain Glenn Miller. "He then gave the assurance that any leading civilian artists the unit needed – people such as Bebe and Ben Lyon, Tommy Trinder, Ted Ray, and Arthur Askey – would be there for the asking.

The new team of 'semi-civilians' had a lot to digest but not much time to take it in. They launched the network within 48 hours and kept it going for the next nine months. Bunks were provided in the basement of Broadcasting House for those who needed to snatch a nap while keeping the forces encouraged and entertained over a testing phase of the war.

Robert Farnon, a fellow Canadian, who was in charge of the Canadian Band, was in the early stages of his career as a great composer, arranger and conductor of light music. He also became a lifelong friend, who often conducted orchestras that Ted sang with.

Ted recalls: "By the end of the war we had done scores of broadcasts together and he was a great companion, although he was also a firm leader. I so enjoyed his wicked sense of humour; he could tell the sauciest stories with the aplomb and innocence of an Archbishop. Once, in winter and in wartime, we had done a concert in a cinema in Barnsley and the promised train to take us back to London did not appear. With the band and extra singers there must have been 100 freezing bodies on the station platform.

"Bob cheerfully cajoled rail staff into producing an engine and some cattle trucks (lined with clean straw!) into which we loaded instruments and ourselves for our journey south. We crowded together for warmth (no hardship as some of the singers were attractive ATS girls!) and he kept morale high along the way with singalongs and a string of close-to-the-knuckle, but never offensive, stories."

Towards the end of the war, Ted was told he should report to RAF Cosford in the Midlands where he was to do training and take exams with a view to receiving a commission. It was a tough time, as he was not at peak fitness; the unrelenting drill and regime of battle courses, using live ammunition, was meant to test potential officers to the limit. There was no mercy. One day Ted slipped while climbing a rope bridge and tore muscles round his ribs. After having his chest taped up he was ordered back on the course.

By the time the war ended he was Pilot Officer Hockridge, and while his fellow Canadians were returning home to be demobbed or continue their military careers, Ted was give a special privilege, courtesy of the military authorities in Ottawa. He was allowed to be demobbed in Britain, on the BBC's promise of immediate radio contracts, and became a full-time singing civvy – and an honorary Brit!

§ § §

CHAPTER 5

"Wait! Those tonsils will have to come out if you want to be a successful singer"

The war was over at last and Ted, now 26, was at a crossroads. He swapped his air force uniform for a grey demob suit. Work awaited him at the BBC but he was uncertain about his plans for the future, and sometimes wondered about the future of his marriage. Back home in Canada, the family, who had followed Ted's progress through letters but who had yet to meet his wife and child, were expecting him to return but he now felt very independent after living in Britain for so long and having experienced so much. Professionally, he had also gained great confidence from mixing with British variety stars and singing with top bands.

One day he was called to the BBC and it was explained that there were rather too many 'Teds' around, in the world of radio entertainment, among them Ted Ray and Ted Andrews (Julie Andrews' father). Ted was asked for his proper Christian name. He told them that it was Edmund and their reaction was: "Perfect!"; for the listeners, this good old Anglo Saxon name would clearly distinguish him from other Teds.

So Ted began to sing regularly with the Queen's Hall Light Orchestra, with the George Melachrino Band, and Geraldo. Then, one day, a telegram arrived offering him a radio contract back in Canada. It was tempting, as the radio show, with full orchestra, would go out coast to coast – and the annual fee would be $10,000. This was a magnificent sum in those days and so, after discussing the options with the BBC, he decided to accept. He sold the house in Britain and Eileen moved in with her parents for the time being.

For the journey home, Ted got a berth on an aircraft carrier that had been transporting food to the UK. Sailing from Liverpool up the Irish Sea, he spotted a mass of lights on the English coastline. Asking which town this was he was told it was the famous seaside resort of Blackpool. Ten years later, he would be entertaining thousands of holiday-makers there in summer seasons.

During the voyage he enjoyed the company of other Canadians returning home, and savoured the on-board food that was a big improvement on the still-limited fare that had been available in Britain immediately after the war. Arriving in Montreal, he went out with some of the officers and indulged in the luxury of four eggs – one of the most memorable meals of his life as, for years, eggs had been a rare treat.

When Ted had settled himself in Toronto, he sent for Eileen and his young son Ian to come and join him. She flew into New York and, having bought a new car, he motored down to meet her. They enjoyed a scenic drive through New England and back to Toronto where Ted soon re-established himself with his coast-to-coast radio series. His career took off and after a year he was voted the most popular singer on Canadian radio.

At this time, two highly enjoyable concerts performing with the Toronto Symphony Orchestra, and featuring songs from Oklahoma!, whetted Ted's appetite for musicals. There was something magical he felt about singing songs from musicals and getting feedback from a live audience.

His indecisiveness about the direction his career should take was not helped when he met an elderly Italian who had been one of Gigli's coaches in Milan and who had told Ted "I think you should be in opera". Ted, following his inspired guidance and coaching over the following months began performing the roles of the Don in Don Giovanni, Marcello in La Boheme in stage productions, and, on coast-to-coast radio, Pizzaro in Fidelio and Captain Bolstrode in Peter Grimes. Benjamin Britten was in Canada at the time and heard the performance.

§ § §

But while his world of music was flourishing, his marriage was proving slightly uneasy. Subtle differences between Eileen and Ted were showing and, in an attempt to patch things up, they came back to England for a holiday. Ted eagerly attended a performance of Oklahoma! at the Theatre Royal, Drury Lane, with Harold Keel (later Howard) playing the lead. He was enthralled.

Ted had to return to Canada to fulfil contracts in Toronto but Eileen chose to stay at home. Carousel had opened on Broadway and some time after arriving in Canada, he flew from Toronto to see it, pronouncing the show – and John Raitt's performance as Billy Bigelow "a knock-out". The role of Billy fascinated him, as it reminded him of characters he had encountered in his youth. Then the inevitable happened. After about three months on his own in Toronto, he started an affair with a beautiful girl on the staff of the Canadian Broadcasting Corporation. She was in her early twenties, very sensual, and from a nice family. It was a torrid physical affair and, although he found it very exciting, Ted soon realised that the relationship had no future.

They came to a mutual agreement to end it and parted friends after six months. Ted, still feeling the responsibility of fatherhood, asked Eileen and Ian to rejoin him in an attempt to hold the marriage together, although he still felt unsure about the future.

During these months of intensive singing in CBC productions, in opera and in several of the Gilbert and Sullivan patter roles he had learned while studying in England with George Baker, Ted began to feel some discomfort in his throat and was recommended to see a Toronto doctor for a check-up.The Polish-Canadian doctor in question turned out to be a brilliant but eccentric ear, nose and throat surgeon. Ted says : "Although I had had my tonsils out as a little boy of four, they had partially grown back and I had not realised that I was just about to have an incredible and somewhat awesome experience…"

During the examination the doctor suddenly shouted: "Wait! Those tonsils must come out if you are to be a success as a singer!" To Ted's consternation he added: "We'll do it now".

Before Ted could protest, the eager medic had frozen the back of Ted's throat with his needle, snipped the tonsils out and nipped off the uvula at the same time, having judged it to be too long. The post-operative treatment was equally cavalier – just a handful of aspirin chewing gum. He bade Ted goodbye and left him to drive himself home. No harm was done; Ted was back singing in two weeks – a credit to instant surgery. Maybe the dynamic doctor was ahead of his time!

CHAPTER 6

"A risky trip, maybe total madness... driving a Hillman Minx across the breadth of America"

With the start of what was seen as an era of promise, and better times – 1950 – Ted increasingly felt that he had to take his career to the next step. Geographically Canada was massive, but the population was so widely dispersed and large venues so few there were limitations for a singer who had ambition. It seemed to Ted – now 31, an age at which dreams can easily slip away – that his future lay elsewhere. Having made his mark at home with his outstanding voice, being voted the most popular singer in Canada, and winning a major radio award, the obvious next destination seemed to be America. Yet he felt that Britain – a country he had grown to love during war service– held the most promise.

At various points in his early career it would have been so easy for Ted to have looked south, to the USA, instead of England, for a career path. A Canadian friend, the actor Lorne Green – who was to have a big hit as the lead actor in TV's Bonanza – was making his way in the States, and encouraged Ted to try his luck over the border. But there were inner doubts, and when, some years later, Ted was at the height of his fame in Britain, he would resist pressure, and the lure of riches, to take the route that was to lead to fortunes for British exports Tom Jones and Engelbert Humperdinck.

Ted was reassured by the popularity he had found as a wartime radio entertainer in Britain, and Bernard Braden, son of a Vancouver clergyman, seemed to be prospering as an actor in England. The only way to find out one way or another was to make the break. After all, selling up and moving on was nothing new in a huge country that was built by people who, in the main, had come from somewhere else.

His father had done it forty years before. One Spring, Charles Hockridge had upped and left Toronto with his wife and family, lured by better prospects. Although Vancouver was Ted's home city, Toronto – where he had been working for the Canadian Broadcasting Corporation – was the departure point of Ted's own trek, which he was to make with Eileen, and young son Ian. Theirs, too, was a Springtime expedition. But there was a difference. His father and family and travelled by train, cooking on the communal stove and reaching the swinging bunk beds on rope ladders. Ted's journey – which turned into a longer-than-expected

3,500-mile cross-country epic – was by car, and their overnight accommodation was in new-fangled sleepover spots called motels.

Curiously – and with a show of cockeyed optimism – the car was not a roomy American sedan, built for long journeys through the wide open spaces but a Hillman Minx, designed for England's suburban roads, a choice that reflected Ted's fondness for Britain and things British. No matter, evidently, that it would have taken a few buckets of luck to find spare parts if it seized up in the Badlands of Dakota, or on one of countless other deserted stretches of road where the passing of another vehicle was a sight to remark on in those days.

But then Ted, by his own admission had, so far – been a lucky fellow. He had been born into a family where there was security, humour and love a-plenty, in beautiful surroundings, and had inherited the musical genes that ran through the family. His infant voice may have given a hint of the boon of an outstanding natural gift (his response, later in life – to those who remarked on the power of his delivery – was that he had been a baritone at six weeks. "I seemed to miss the boy soprano phase!" he says). Ted's added good fortune lay in the fact that there were people around him who appreciated the potential of what they heard and – in churches and choirs, and around the family piano – they encouraged him to sing. Not that he needed much encouragement; he was doing what came naturally.

He would hear Laurence Tibbet singing on the radio, or even live in Vancouver and sit in his bathtub later trying to find the same sound. Often he would stride out alone among the towering firs and burst into a Nelson Eddy number he had heard on the radio, or a traditional ballad. He has often remarked that singing among the trees was like singing in a cathedral. Singing in church choirs and at local musical events led to solo work and the recognition that his voice was something special. Confirmation had now come through roles in opera, operetta and a burgeoning career on radio, the magical medium that – in those pre-TV days – had first carried into his home the voices of singers of world renown.

§ § §

As Ted and Eileen arranged to sell their Toronto home, and just about everything else except Ted's precious music and piano – which was shipped ahead to England – Ted was aware that the move to Britain would not only be a further testing ground for his career but also for his marriage. Even with good intentions and goodwill on both sides, and with the bonding influence of a young son, the relationship was not all it might have been, something that saddened Ted, who, as a self-confessed romantic, had an unfulfilled need for a soul-mate, something more than the 'good wife' Eileen had always been, and always remained.

It was only later in life, when he found the love of his life, that he was able to see his first marriage with clarity, and understand where it had been lacking.

Embarking on what Ted, in retrospect, called "our risky trip, maybe total madness", the family set off, the Minx tootling from Toronto to Detroit, up Michigan state, beneath Lake Superior and to Grand Forks, North Dakota, where the plan was to head north to Winnipeg to see brother Brick. But the Red River was flooding so they had to pick their way to Vancouver by heading south to Fargo, real Wild West country, and turning west through North Dakota and Montana. There they diverted to take in the Yellowstone National Park and broke the journey with some family fun, going fly-fishing and spotting wildlife everywhere, elk, moose, buffalo, and bears. Ian had been taken canoeing when the family lived in Toronto, so he relished this wilderness of gurgling geysers and exciting animals.

On reaching Vancouver, having called to gaze in wonder at the Grand Coulee Dam, and motored up to Alberta, and finally through the Canadian Rockies, Ted sold the Minx to Brick. There were more than 3,500 more miles on the clock than when they had set off from Toronto. The family boarded a Royal Mail Line refrigerator ship that offered an attractive deal to a dozen passengers who travelled in first class comfort. The adventures in ports along the way came free.

Ted has many memories of that 10,000-mile voyage, with 11 other first-class passengers enjoying excellent meals with the captain and officers, comfortable cabins, and even a small swimming pool that gave

Ted the chance to teach Ian to swim. They had a quick trip ashore at San Diego, California, where Ted was the only passenger on the first run of the day on the world's highest big dipper, and partied with champagne on the top deck as they went through the Panama Canal.

At Curacao, while Ted was swimming with some of the officers in a shark-proof beach area, a deep dive revealed that the steel netting protecting them had a hole in it big enough to let a whale through, let alone a shark (there was an immediate mass exodus!). Especially memorable for Ted, as a nature lover, were the whales and dolphins that cavorted round the bow of the ship as they crossed the Atlantic.

When the ship docked at Plymouth, the family travelled to join Eileen's family at their house in Kent. They were disembarking into a country, which, despite worries over the war in Korea, continuing rationing, and the UK having just suffered the wettest winter for 80 years, was struggling for a brighter and better future. Car ownership was rising quickly, Ark Royal was being launched, the Festival of Britain was being planned – and, often, children weren't! The birth rate had boomed with the return of thousands of servicemen and former prisoners of war.

Many people were also tidying up their lives. Divorce figures soared as couples concluded relationships broken by long separation, or infidelity, or those formed on shifting ground in the precarious days of war. It was a country hungry for glamour and upbeat entertainment to counter the shortages and rationing still lingering five years after war ended. This was to be a fertile ground for spectacular stage musicals which were bursting with colour, energy, drama and romance, in such contrast to the daily mainstay of BBC radio which at that time took pride in excluding regional accents, keeping po-faced and censoring sauciness.

Ted and Eileen continued to work on their marriage. They had a flat and Ted resumed contact with people he knew at the BBC to explore ways of taking his talent in new directions. He appeared on Henry Hall's Guest Night and was a regular on Strike Up The Music. But there were better things just around the corner. That fateful phone call from Teddy Holmes told Ted of the Carousel auditions. Within a couple of days his life had been transformed.

The fight scene in Carousel with me as Billy Bigelow.

 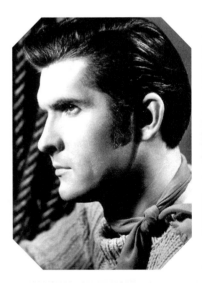

Playing dead with Laverne Burden... and in character as Billy

A portrait taken in Toronto in the late Forties

I took just one look at this girl and fell in love with her instantly – and I still am 50 years later!

The opening mime scene of Carousel. When I was asked to help restage the show with new people for the tour, my eyes met Jackie's for the first time.

CHAPTER 7

"I felt for Billy, this hard man who was basically a softy pouring out his thoughts on forthcoming fatherhood"

It was a little ironic that after travelling 13,000 miles to London, rather than going to America to further his career, Ted Hockridge, a Canadian, should find himself in one of Britain's finest and oldest theatres rehearsing to play an American.

A whole new world was opening up to him as he rehearsed the role with the support of the cast and of Stephen Douglas who he was to replace. Years later Douglas revealed that he had gone into the back of the circle to watch Ted's first trial matinee performance and had been very impressed with his singing and the way he had interpreted the character of Billy Bigelow. He was also struck by how alike he and Ted looked, an opinion confirmed by the photographs in the show brochure. These were a mix of pictures of the two leads but show-goers had to look hard to see which Billy was which.

The Theatre Royal, Drury Lane, was granted a Royal Charter in 1665 by King Charles I I and here he was centre stage in a show that would run and run, with every seat sold. As Ted said later: "I could just see the great David Garrick staring down at me from 'up there' and saying: 'Who is that Canadian brat in my No 1 dressing room?' "

It was clear that the part he had won was perfect for Ted. The character of Billy Bigelow, the fairground barker, called for imposing stature, matched by vocal strength, coupled with acting ability. It also required stamina, especially for the Soliloquy that lasts seven minutes, what one theatre critic called "an astonishing scene", where Billy is called on to sing the emotions of an expectant father. Although Ted had never had acting lessons, opera – especially his roles as lead in Don Giovanni and Marcello in La Boheme – had given him some ability to "become" someone else, and take on their personality and emotions.

George Baker's coaching for Gilbert and Sullivan roles also reinforced Ted's confidence in being able to portray characters. Additionally, he had seen all sorts of dramatic productions as a boy with his parents who loved theatre – and he believes that the real-life drama he experienced in Canada helped him to envisage how to put over dramatic scenes. He says:

"The Billy Bigelow character – a raunchy, swaggering fairground character, was totally familiar to me. I had met many of his sort at the

Vancouver Exhibition where I worked in my teens in the cattle section every year. At the big show, the daytime activities were followed by fun at the fairground at night. I knew the type well.

"I felt for Billy, this hard man who was basically a softy at heart, pouring out his innermost thoughts on forthcoming fatherhood. The Soliloquy was everything I could have hoped for both vocally and dramatically".

There was something emotionally uplifting about Carousel, so affecting that 50 years afterwards, fans could recall how it felt to be in the audience. Even critics who prided themselves on being aloof from the sentiment that musicals could stir within the audience, had to admit to finding that the Rodgers score – which the composer believed to be his finest – and the Hammerstein lyrics got to them. One confessed in print: "This critic came out with his hard-boiled shell quite stripped away and his heart and mind exalted."

John Hanson, a tenor whose lead roles in such traditional touring musicals as Desert Song and the Student Prince, both written in the Twenties, had made him a British institution, remarked at the time on the emergence of big characters with big voices – none of them tenors – in the new musicals of the Fifties, and picked out Ted Hockridge as typifying the new breed. He would have agreed with the description of one theatre pundit who had remarked that Ted's physical presence made him appear to be "the sort of guy who could sing a lullaby while sawing a tree". Hanson said: "That role fitted him like a glove."

Most theatre critics agreed that the mysterious man out there in the dark at the auditions had got the right man. One journalist came out of the show and wrote: "One personality dominates Carousel, and that is Edmund Hockridge as Billy Bigelow, the ne'er-do-well fairground barker who attempts to redeem in the shadowy after-world his real-life failures. He is that rare combination of a fine singer and accomplished actor."

Ted recalls the sense of surprise, and even shock, that overtook him when, as he worked out movements on stage and learned his cues, it finally sank in that he had secured the role and would be appearing on the massive Theatre Royal stage every day for many months; it was clear that the public support for Carousel would not wane in the foreseeable future.

"I was stunned by what was happening to me. It was all so new and it all happened so quickly but my confidence grew daily," Ted recalls.

What was most satisfying was that he was using what he had been given – a superb voice – and what he had learned, especially vocal projection.

The Theatre Royal, with its 2,000-plus seats, was big but Ted's voice was a match for it. It reached every corner and the audience could hear every word. What's more he had the stamina to do it time and time again; in fact, he was to sing the demanding role of Billy more than 1,100 times. That means that he sang the Soliloquy for the equivalent of more than 28 hours during the London run, and national tour, of Carousel!

The triumph of the show and his part in it had a bitter counterpoint. Ted and Eileen were still persevering, clinging on to their marriage. Another child was expected but in fact this was to add to their desolation. After one matinee, in the late summer, when Ted had been in Carousel for a few months, he received a phone call to say that Ian now had a baby brother. Sadly, the baby lived for only two days. Ted pulled out of the show with the shock and, after taking a week away to recover, he returned to perform for the rest of the run before the planned national tour.

Back in the 1950s marriages that broke up usually had to have a culprit and a victim; this was how the divorce courts worked. There was little room for what fifty years later was the norm, the belief that it took two to make a bargain and, if it was broken, rarely was it simply a case of one being the transgressor and the other the victim. Marriages were more complicated than that.

At the basis of Ted's marriage was, he believes, not failure of either partner but simply irreconcilable difference in needs, especially as Ted's career began to take off and, as he admits, he became consumed by his Carousel role, immersed in a character that asked so much of him each day. When he describes Eileen it is not critically but as someone with admirable qualities: "She was a good mother, a good wife and a strong support. And although I could not be totally happy I did not want to hurt anyone and had tried to be a good husband and supportive father.

"If I had been totally honest with myself, I suppose I should never have married. But because I knew Eileen loved me, and because I did not want to cause hurt deliberately, it made it all the more difficult for me to admit that I had never felt the same about her."

Growing celebrity status meant that Ted's opportunities were widening. His first recording was for HMV, appropriately enough for an anglophile who had returned to Britain, and was making it his home, was *I Leave My Heart In An English Garden*. This became a great favourite and was often played on air. Then came recording sessions for Parlophone, with a recording manager called George Martin, just in his twenties then, years before he became the architect of The Beatles recording phenomenon.

Ted's appreciation of the historical side of Britain was strong and, in an amusing incident during a performance of Carousel, he believed he was seeing part of our ghostly heritage. It was believed that a bewigged ghost inhabited the Theatre Royal. During the matinee, when Billy Bigelow and the low-life Jigger, being played by Morgan Davies, face each other for a tense confrontation on the dockside, the angry dialogue came to an abrupt halt.

Ted, as Billy, waited for Jigger's next line, but the cue never came. Instead, Jigger stared wildly past Billy and up at the Royal Box on the opposite side of the stage. He began to shake.

"What's wrong?" Ted demanded to know in a whisper, barely moving his mouth. Jigger muttered: "The ghost! It's the bloody ghost!"

Ted quickly ad-libbed with a bit of extra dialogue, rose from the hay bale he had been sitting on, and sauntered nonchalantly around Jigger to try to look at what Jigger had seen without bringing the entire show to a halt.

Sure enough, there was a white-wigged and ghostly figure wearing attire from centuries back, sitting in the semi-darkness of the Queen's private box. Billy and Jigger somehow completed the scene realistically before Jigger rushed off to his dressing room aghast over the spectre of the 'Ghost of Drury Lane', an apparition that was said to be linked with a skeleton, with a knife in its ribs, that had been found a century before in a bricked up part of the theatre.

The truth turned out to be less spooky. Way back in the 17th century, patrons had been welcomed into the foyer by a colourfully-costumed and bewigged footman, and since the tradition had been maintained. Jigger had not seen a ghost – just a 1950s footman in his antique outfit enjoying a nap in a cosy corner of the royal box, out of the sight of the audience.

It was as a result of the fight scene with Jigger, in which Billy is stabbed to death, that Ted sustained a real injury. Every time he was 'killed', Ted would fall onto one side and although 'repetitive strain injury' was unknown at the time, the constant falling was pushing his hip out of kilter. A renowned osteopath, Kenneth Underhill, was recommended and would keep the Hockridge torso in shape for another half century.

During the last five weeks of Carousel's Drury Lane run, South Pacific was preparing to move in. The stage of the Theatre Royal is so huge that the scenery for both shows could be set and hung, South Pacific on the back and Carousel on the front half. The new show rehearsed throughout the day, and Carousel took the stage for evening performances. As Ted recalls: "I frequently came in early to enjoy the rehearsals which had Mary Martin in the lead, as well as two interesting newcomers in the chorus of the sailors singing There Is Nothing Like A Dame. One was Mary Martin's son, Larry Hagman, later to star in Dallas on TV as J.R. Ewing and the other a striking young Scot who told me: "I'm not really a singer you know, I'm an actor". And that was Sean Connery.

Ted quickly adjusted to the attention his growing fame brought, and his tolerance extended to the most testing of strangers who approached him. And anyway, there will always be someone out there who will try to cut you down to size.

Once, at a golf club, he was confronted by a member whose slurred speech left no doubt that he had enjoyed all the refreshments available at the 19th hole. Approaching Ted, he said triumphantly: "I know you…(burp). You were in Oklahoma!" Ted replied, "No, I wasn't."

"Oh, yes you were."

"No," Ted replied: "You are thinking of Howard Keel."

"No….I know you…. you were in Oklahoma…."

"No," Ted insisted. "I'm Edmund Hockridge and I was in Carousel."

"Ah," said the drunk momentarily nonplussed. "Well…" he said after a moment's fuddled thought. "Well, I didn't like YOU either!"

You can't win 'em all!

CHAPTER 8

"I came onto the stage between shows, Ted came out and saw me and we spoke for the first time"

After its phenomenal Drury Lane run, Carousel was about to hit the road. It was booked into more than 30 of the leading theatres throughout Britain for varying stays, the longest, in Manchester, for six weeks. Ted Hockridge, in more than 1,100 performances, had made the part of Billy Bigelow his own; his growing fame would help it to maintain its record in the provinces as a sell-out show. It was now September, 1951, and Ted received a message asking him to attend pre-tour rehearsals at the Stoll Theatre, Kingsway, so that newcomers to the cast could work round the central characters in the show's seven-minute mime section of the fairground scene.

Arriving at the theatre, he was not sure where he was expected to be, and inadvertently walked into a dance rehearsal room where a beautiful young woman was limbering up at the bar. She had red hair, and the lovely legs of a dancer but it was the eyes that held Ted riveted to the spot for a moment before he moved off.

For many months Ted had been surrounded by beautiful young singers and dancers and with his good looks, engaging personality, and a singing voice that – as the critics had said – could send shivers down the back of anyone who heard it, he could have been forgiven for playing the field. In fact, it was acknowledged among the cast that trying to win him over was time wasted as he was totally dedicated to his career.

People could be forgiven for wondering how a man who, in the words of one critic had "a voice of virility and charm and the sort of looks young ladies want to encounter on the beach", could capitalising on his enviable position, espcailly as he had a somewhat shaky marriage.

The two-year national tour of Carousel was underway, beginning in south London, at the Streatham Hill Theatre. During the show the couple's eyes met again. Neither of them spoke. As Ted waited for his entry at scene changes, across the stage would be the girl, awaiting her entry. If they passed on the staircase they looked at each other meaningfully, yet again, nothing was said. Ted's leading lady, Jane Martin, had spotted the girl and remarked on her beauty, but Ted did not need to be told. He was transfixed.

§ § §

CHAPTER EIGHT

One day, in between shows, Ted passed a coffee shop and, glancing in, he saw the dancer. She was with a distinguished-looking man in his late twenties. He was looking intense, in fact he was serious about the girl. She wasn't but Ted was not to know that. They had still not spoken. Whatever Ted felt at that moment was disturbing enough for him to say to himself: "Now watch it, son…calm your thoughts man."

Two weeks later, when the show moved to Golders Green, he learned how right he was to feel that he needed to put on the brakes – and just how helpless he was to stop whatever they were on the verge of moving them forward into freefall. Jacqueline – Jackie Jefferson – had broken down the barriers, and the smiles that radiated from both of them when they met again at the theatre told the story.

Jackie herself remembers the moment when the glances and the smiles that had been the overture to their meeting led inevitably to something more. "I came down on to the stage between shows, at around tea-time, to do some warming up. Ted's dressing room was at stage level. He came out and saw me and we spoke for the first time."

He invited her into his dressing room and there was an embrace and a tender kiss.

Ted learned that Jackie, a Brighton girl, was travelling in for the show each day with another girl, Terry Donovan, a friend who gone to the same school and who was also a young dancer in Brighton. Jackie had made up her mind to be a dancer even before that, when she attended Molly Ball's dance classes, and her dream came true when, at 16, she made her professional debut at the Brighton Hippodrome in a panto starring Max Wall. Within a year she was in Bless the Bride in London, as a dancer, with Terry, and two years later they had secured places on the Carousel tour.

Jackie says: "Although I was a sexually normal girl who was just turning 19 when I joined the cast of Carousel, I was also a romantic with high ideals of retaining my virginity until I got married. I had had several boyfriends, none of them serious, and was always attracted to an older man; the younger ones seemed to bore me. But I was beginning to wonder whether I would ever really fall in love.

"All that changed very quickly when my own eyes locked on those hazel eyes gazing across the stage, burning through me, as we stared at each other while waiting for our individual entries. Suddenly the dormant flame within me was set alight. But a married man with a son had not been planned. At the time neither of us thought of the circumstances. For my part I was totally smitten."

Ted volunteered to give Jackie and Terry a lift to Victoria Station where they caught the train to Brighton each night. On the way Ted and Jackie touched each other's hands on the gearshift: Terry, in the back, was oblivious of the electrical charge between the two.

Ted was 13 years older than Jackie who was just 19. But age did not seem to matter at that moment; even so early in their relationship there was a certainty that this was the real thing. Ted recalls: "To be 32 and to be feeling like that for the first time in my life was amazing. I knew that this was what I wanted and what I'd been waiting for. Of course, there was a lingering guilt but I'd been a good father and tried to hold things together and somehow what was happening seemed so innocent and so right."

As a graceful and beautiful young woman, Jackie had been the target of male attention; in fact a boy friend would wait each night to meet her at the Brighton station. But she had no feelings for him. Other suitors – among them an orchestra conductor and a love-struck oboist – had failed to impress, and the wealthy Irish businessman who had followed Bless the Bride around the country in the hope of winning Jackie over, found he was on a fruitless quest. "After three or four weeks of knowing someone I grew bored and had begun to think that I would never feel serious about anybody," says Jackie.

During the war, a Canadian unit, The Lake Superior regiment, was attached to her father's Oxford and Buckinghamshire Light Infantry regiment in Brighton. He brought many of these Canadians home to extend hospitality. In return, they brought wonderful food parcels with them for the family. From then on, young Jackie had a soft spot for Canadians and for Canada. Terry remained unaware of the growing bond between Jackie and Ted. Each night they would have a lift from Ted – once having to get out and push the car out of the snow – and settle down on the late-night Brighton train that was used regularly by other theatre professionals such as Jimmy Edwards.

Jackie would shut her eyes and pretend to be asleep; in fact, she would spend the journey day-dreaming about Ted. She smiles at her memory of a camp character who, getting on the train and seeing her feigning sleep, chirruped: "Ooh, darling – perchanth to dream!." Waiting for her at the end of the journey, as always, would be the dutiful boy friend, and waiting for Ted would be Eileen, both unaware of the secret only Ted and Jackie shared.

After the show had played the Liverpool Empire for three weeks, during which time Ted and Jackie learned more and more about each other, Carousel arrived at the Lyceum, Edinburgh, for a five-week run spanning Christmas.

Eileen and Ian, now seven, travelled up for a festive season that was controlled and cool rather than celebratory. Ted and Jackie were having to act both on and off the stage. The theatre manager invited Jackie to be his partner at a New Year's ball. He was gallant and attentive and gave Jackie an orchid corsage but her mind was somewhere else, and her eyes on Ted's as they caught sight of each other before the ball.

Their romance, that had only just begun, was put in jeopardy when Carousel arrived at His Majesty's Theatre, Aberdeen. The Winter was bitter and the iron stage hard and unrelenting. Jackie, who had not warmed up as she normally did, tore the cartilage in her knee as she dropped to the stage in a knee-fall which was part of the "June Dance" sequence that follows *June Is Busting Out All Over*.

It was a serious injury, and one that would normally have meant that the show would have to call in a new dancer. If that had happened, Ted and Jackie might not have seen each other again, a thought neither of them could contemplate. But Jackie had become understudy to the Mrs Snow character, and was not easily replaced, so she was given time to recover and for the muscle in her thigh, which had begun to waste from lack of use, to be built up.

fter several weeks at the Kings Theatre, Glasgow, the rigours of the
ish winter were easing and the show moved to the Grand Theatre,
s. So far, Edmund and Jackie had not had a date as such. But
suddenly, it was Spring! They arranged a day out and for the sake of
discretion they agreed to meet at the bus station, with the idea of visiting
Ripon. They were so in love, and happy to be together, that it might have
been a Rolls Royce taking them to the Ritz rather than a bus taking them
to a little market town. They canoodled like teenagers on the back seat
and enjoyed an unforgettable day together.

On another trip, to Knaresborough, they went into a pub for lunch
and the landlord, believing himself to be a pianist, tried to provide
romantic music as a background to their tryst but he might as well have
been playing in boxing gloves. They were hysterical as Some Enchanted
Evening was performed mainly on the cracks between the keys and with
half the bars missing, as Ted laughingly tried to serenade Jackie.

As all couples do, they were gathering shared experiences, the funny,
memorable and sometimes moving moments that underpin a
relationship, and which in future years provide the material for fond
reminiscence. One such moment was a trip Ted and Jackie made to York
where their feelings of being on top of the world were enhanced by the
heady pleasure of going to the top of York Minster. They travelled north
with a host of Yorkshire memories to cherish for the rest of their lives.

The next stop for Carousel was Newcastle, followed by a long run in
Manchester. Here the favoured digs for show people were with a Mrs
McKay. When her Carousel guests arrived Mrs McKay, with her trained
eye, seemed to sense that there might be something going on between
Ted and Jackie, so, following a long tradition of landladies who doubled as
moral guardians, she ensured that Jackie was put out of harm's way in an
annexe. Obviously she had not heard of the saying 'Love will find a way'
– and it did, with Terry's help! Mrs McKay, who, incidentally, had the
knack of choosing precisely the wrong word to express what she wanted
to say, never knew the ghastly truth and went on blithely welcoming more
showbiz clients. Some of them – as two guests, Billy Dainty and Joan

Regan recalled – were once promised that on their next visit they would find "muriels on the walls and illuminated pelvises".

§ § §

There were other comical – and unintended – moments during the tour…

After the show had been on tour for some months, Bill Footer, who played the part of the policeman, and who had been on the receiving end of some good-natured practical jokes dreamed up by Ted, decided to take his revenge. It was a dull, mid-winter matinee and the show had reached the scene – a very serious one – when Julie enters with a cup of coffee for her husband, Billy, and is about to tell him that he is to become a father. Ted was blissfully unaware that on this occasion the 'coffee' had been heavily spiked with Oxo and pepper.

Julie made her exit, and, on cue Mrs Mullins arrived. Ted sipped his 'coffee' and choked, throwing the rest of the brew towards the 'Laughing Policeman' and other giggling members of the cast, enjoying his discomfort from the wings. Trying to compose himself, he told Mrs Mullins that he is about to become a father. Mocking him, she turned to exit, and Ted – as the enraged Billy – "kicked" her offstage as usual, with the line "Goodbye, Mrs Mullins!". But this time, as he launched into his kick, his other foot slipped in the spilt coffee – and he fell flat on his backside with a bump. Unfortunately he then had to go immediately into the dramatic seven-minute Soliloquy. Somehow his nerve held, and he was able to carry off the scene, and he often wondered whether to the audience his undignified fall had been planned into the staging of the show.

When Carousel moved south, to Bournemouth Pavilion Theatre, Ted had a chance to indulge in a boyhood passion – sailing. A character called Chub Keynes had a boatyard at Mudeford and from there Ted took Jackie out into Christchurch Bay for a sailing lesson in a dinghy. They sailed towards Christchurch Ledge an area famous for bass fishing. They were blissfully alone, a rare pleasure, and as the boat bobbed in the bay they did not hesitate to show some – but not all! – of the passion they felt for each other. They were well out of range of the rest of humanity; after all, the nearest building was the Needles lighthouse, about a mile away.

Somewhat reluctantly they returned to land, and down to earth. Chub was waiting for them. "Where have you been?" he asked, mischievously. "We had a call from the lighthouse keeper who had been using his binoculars and seen the most amazing things happening in a dinghy out there…"

Neither Jackie nor Ted knew what the future would hold, although their bond was growing stronger and the likelihood of them parting seemed remote now, and too painful to contemplate. Yet Ted was still married, and although he sensed that Eileen knew that there was someone new in his life, nothing was said. Ted, who, like most servicemen, had smoked during the war, was then still a smoker, and when Jackie wanted to buy him a special gift she chose a cigarette case and had the word 'Pact' inscribed in it so that when he was not with her he would remember the pledge that their relationship implied; they were together and would be in the future.

But the path ahead was littered with thorny problems. They ran into the first very quickly when Eileen found the cigarette case and was confronted with tangible evidence of something that she already suspected.

Ted and Jackie met for lunch in Rottingdean, near Brighton, to talk and decide on the best way forward. They knew Eileen would be badly hurt. On top of that Ted had Ian to consider, and they themselves were finding the insecurity of their affair painful. There seemed to be no winners. Parting was an option but even discussing it was so agonising that they found themselves in tears. Finally, the talking had to stop and the action start. They decided with deep sadness that it would be best for everyone involved if they ended the affair.

Perhaps the decision was a test they had set, unconsciously and without acknowledging it, to discover whether they could indeed live without each other.

The result was a dramatic affirmation of their love. Parting was not the solution. Ted had felt nothing but pain and misery and Jackie was bereft as, for almost a week, the stand-off was maintained on both sides.

Ted recalls: "After the worst five days of my life I picked up the phone and told Jackie: 'I'm sorry but I can't live without you'. She replied that she felt the same way about me. We then vowed to spend the rest of our lives together. Jackie knew that it might be years before we were free to marry but we had now made a commitment and she was prepared to wait as long as it took."

It was time to come clean with Eileen. Ted told her the truth and, even though for weeks she had suspected that what she was now hearing had been going on, understandably, she was devastated. "She was brave, and tried hard to recover from it. She began to realise that I could not be happy without Jackie and she began to get on with her own life," says Ted. A mutual agreement was reached to try to shield Ian from the effects of the break-up.

Of course, divorce in those days often produced sensational coverage, unlike today when most divorces go unrecorded by the Press. The decision was that there would be no divorce until Ian, now a boarder at a public school in Sussex, had reached the age of 16.

§ § §

Despite the personal problems, the show went on – as it always must – and audiences were unaware of the romantic link between Ted and Jackie. There were many happy moments spent together, even though they felt guilt and frustration that they could not immediately be acknowledged as a couple. Inevitably there were also comical incidents on the tour, even times when the dramatic continuity of Carousel was threatened by something unexpected and hilarious!

One occurred on a rainy night in Southsea, during Billy's fight scene with Jigger. In this Billy is stabbed and falls dead on a bale of straw. The challenge for Ted when he was learning the part was to develop a technique of shallow breathing that allowed him to lie motionless for nine minutes while the action goes on around him. The whole scene relies on

Billy being a convincing corpse, and Ted, during scores of performances, had long since perfected a way of stopping his chest and diaphragm from moving even slightly.

Playing dead for so long was a tough enough test for any actor. But on this occasion, at the Kings's Theatre, there was the additional difficulty of coping with the Chinese water torture that bedevilled this particular performance. For as Ted settled down to being dead, a drop of water pinged onto his forehead, followed by another… and he knew he had nine minutes more of lying directly beneath a slow cascade of drips coming from the leaking theatre roof!

Ted and Jackie found that a sense of the ridiculous was a blessing and there was an element of farce to what was otherwise a very special and significant moment for both of them, when the sublime and the ridiculous arrived side by side…

Carousel was playing Liverpool for three weeks so Ted and Jackie had time to explore the surroundings. Ted recalls: "We decided to go for a picnic over to Birkenhead peninsula. There we settled down into what we believed to be an isolated field. It was a beautiful Spring day, and we made love. Afterwards we lay in each other's arms and pondered what the future might hold for us. But suddenly we heard the roar of engines everywhere. We had chosen the spot because it was isolated and so – evidently – had the Army who were starting manoeuvres all around us with tanks, motor bikes and jeeps. Literally, the earth moved for us! We dissolved into hysterical laughter, hurled the picnic basket and blankets into the car and managed to beat a hasty retreat, before the attacking forces closed in on us!"

In May of 1953, towards the end of the two-year Carousel tour, came a call from the impresario Prince Littler to say that the Canadian Government wanted Ted to represent Canada in the special choir for the Coronation at Westminster Abbey in the following month. Opera singers Joan Carlysle and Inia Te Wiata would be representing Australia and New Zealand. As ten days of rehearsal of Sir William Walton's music would be needed, Littler decided to take Carousel off the road for two weeks in the build up to the Coronation and over the day itself.

CHAPTER EIGHT

The choir members were from all the different cathedrals of Britain, many of whom had done other Coronations, starting as boy sopranos. Ted recalls: "One very friendly and personable character, from one of the great cathedrals, told me some amusing anecdotes about previous regal occasions. But the funniest happened on the great day itself.

"We had to be at the Abbey at 8am and prepared to go up into the choir loft by 9am as it would take two hours to handle the deadly slow procession of arrivals, and seating most of the congregation. This would lead to the final moment just before 11am when the very top VIPs would arrive, Winston Churchill, Arabian kings, ambassadors and so on.

"So, by the end of the service we would, at the very least, have been in the choir loft for four hours. But I was not so much concerned about that as the fact that my friend seemed to have suddenly put on weight.

"No, my son,'" he said. 'As I told you this is my third coronation – and you learn by experience'." He then pulled up his cassock and revealed a strong leather belt around his midriff. From it hung a large bundle of sandwiches, a small bottle of brandy, a flask of tea, a hot water bottle (to fight off the early morning chill) and… a huge, empty hot water bottle. What a practical and sensible gentleman! Laughingly he pleaded : 'But don't tell the Queen!' "

§ § §

In the role of Sky Masterson, the big-time gambler and hero of the plot of Guys and Dolls

CHAPTER

9

"Dat punch was beautiful, Ted"
said Big Julie after the show.
"Real beautiful"

Unbelievable as it seemed to the cast, soon the music would fade and the Carousel would finally stop turning. By the time the last tour dates were ticked off on the calendar, almost 2.5 million people had seen the show since it opened in London, and many of them never forgot the magical feeling that the score, the singing, the lyrics and the drama combined to leave with them as the house lights went up and they headed home with the anthem, *You'll Never Walk Alone*, still ringing in the ears.

For Ted Hockridge – and for Jackie – the show had become a way of life. Ted had snatched the opportunity of a lifetime, and won fame as a musicals star. But as a realist, he knew he had to start thinking about his future because, lucky as he felt himself to be, he was unlikely to get the offer of another plum role just as Carousel ended its second and last tour. He was wrong. While he waited to go on stage at the Hippodrome, Bristol, a second wonderful role was delivered to his dressing room and dropped at his feet – not by Lady Luck, although as it turned out she had indeed been a lady that night! – but by a couple of straight-talking visitors with clipped Brooklyn accents.

Ted was invited – well, instructed – to sit down and listen. They got straight to the point and within a minute he was silently awe-struck by what was being proposed. "They put me on cloud nine by telling me that they had seen my performance as Billy the night before and they wanted me for the main singing role of the big-time New York gambler in the London production of Guys and Dolls. I thought – 'Wow, me as Sky Masterson, and my second London musical!' "

The more details Ted heard, the better it got. The show was to be staged at the 2,350-seat Coliseum with practically a full concert orchestra in the pit. There would be a cast of 50 or more and nearly all the Broadway leads – Sam Levene, Vivian Blaine, Stubby Kaye, Tom Pedi and Lou Herbert among them – would be in the cast. Ted was to be Sky and Lizbeth Webb his leading lady.

Ted remembers going on stage in a dream that night but he was brought back down to earth next morning. The opening of the Guys and Dolls run was due to start before the Carousel run finished. The overlap was a month, and Prince Littler said he was not prepared to release Ted until Carousel ended its tour.

Then someone in the management trying to secure Ted for Guys and Dolls had a bright idea and rang with a request and a possible solution. Could he look at the rest of his tour dates and work out whether he could continue to appear in Carousel and travel to London each day for Guys and Dolls rehearsals?

Ted recalls "My reply was: 'I sure can!', and then quickly confirmed that the last theatre booking, at Northampton, was about two hours by train to London. In fact, in my eagerness I had totally failed to grasp the pressures and the daily race against time I'd be involved in. But nothing was going to stop me, and Littler finally agreed to the arrangement."

When Guys and Dolls opened in London it was an immediate hit. A stand-in from Broadway played Sky, while Ted learned the part, at the same time performing in Carousel each night. Ted was embarking on the most hectic month of his life. "I would get to bed at midnight after each Carousel performance. I'd have a quick late supper, and grab five hours sleep. I'd scramble into my clothes at 5 am and gulp down a quick breakfast before dashing for the London-bound train to reach St Martin's Lane, near Trafalgar Square, by 9 am at the latest. I would then rehearse in the empty Coliseum until 3 pm and then catch the train back to Northampton. By then it was five-thirty or six o'clock so I just had time for a snack before I climbed into my costume, checked the voice with a scale or two and slipped back into the character of Billy Bigelow."

When Ted finally joined the cast he felt indebted to an American called Jerry Wayne, who had been understudy for the Sky role in New York and who performed it for a month. Ted remembers that although it was hard for Jerry to relinquish the role, he had shown no resentment on leaving it to allow Ted to take over the part that, incidentally, Robert Alda, the father of Alan Alda, of M.A.S. H. fame, had played in the New York production.

Ted's exit from Carousel and his opening in Guys and Dolls were just as frenetic as the rest of the previous month had been. The final performance of Carousel was on a Saturday night but owing to some mismanagement of dates Ted could not snatch any rest before taking on his role as Masterson. In fact, he went straight off to do a BBC radio show on the day after Carousel closed, had a full dress rehearsal with the Guys and Dolls cast during the next day before making his first appearance in the show that night.

Guys and Dolls was described as 'a musical fable of Broadway, based on the stories and characters of Damon Runyan.' Fortuitously, Ted loved the Runyan stories of gangsters and crooks infesting certain areas of Broadway. He had read them all when he was living in Toronto and had brought a collection of them with him when he returned to England. His transformation from Billy Bigelow to Sky Masterson was effortless.

§ § §

Ted immediately struck up a rapport with the cast. He also felt very much at home with Lizbeth Webb, who during the run, sang on I Hear Music, Ted's Home Service radio show. His other guests were Benny Hill, Jimmy Edwards, Petula Clark, the teenage Julie Andrews – and Bernard Braden, Ted's former Vancouver neighbour.

Most of Ted's Guys and Dolls memories are of the fun he had, and of the hilarious incidents that added to the joy of being in another musical that was the talk of the town. It was a happy show, with some memorable songs – *I've Never Been In Love Before, Luck Be A Lady,* and *My Time Of Day* among them – and the Broadway cast was a revelation. Ted was leaving the heavy and intense role of Billy and having to transform himself into the suave gambler, Sky.

Quite often in the crap game scenes on stage the money (and the game) was real; it was their way of keeping the show fresh during what turned out to be another long run. After all, this American company had already played the show for two years in New York before coming over to London. More often than not the public were unaware of the unscripted humour behind the scenes but sometimes they were aware of problems – such as the time that the dressing room Tannoy failed to warn cast members of their imminent entries, causing continuity chaos.

Getting a fit of the giggles was a hazard, and Lizbeth Webb could break up very easily. On the night when the Tannoy broke down she had no chance of controlling herself as more and more of the characters in the plot missed their cues. At this point, as she and Ted were about to go into the romantic duet *I've Never Been In Love Before*, a dialogue gaffe caught her unawares.

The script calls for Sky to reveal that his real name is Obediah Masterson but instead of saying "That's my real name" Ted said: "That's ry meal name" – at which Lizbeth dissolved into chortles. She and Ted then launched into the love song, trying gamely to maintain some semblance of romantic atmosphere but Lizbeth's singing voice had been submerged in stifled laughter. Ted compensated by singing his own part, then raising the pitch of his voice to a mixture of tenor and falsetto to cover for her. The result was an unplanned comic bonus for members of the audience, including Arthur Askey, who told Ted: "That was the funniest thing I've seen in years!"

On another night, Ted, as Sky – the cool gambling dude – was horror-stricken to notice, as he waited to make an entry, that the fly zip of his sharp single-breasted stage suit had burst open and wouldn't stay shut. In a masterly piece of improvisation he borrowed the big bass drum, used by the Salvation Army characters in the show, and went on with it, hiding the all-revealing aperture until the scene finished.

Practical jokes were always a hazard, and when Sid James took over from Sam Levine as Nathan Detroit everyone had to be extra vigilant. Sid's exploits with women are legendary and occasional noises from his dressing room confirmed that his reputation was not misplaced. But he was also wickedly inventive with ideas to cause maximum embarrassment.

One night, Ted went to his dressing room and wondered why the company was gathered in the corridor near the door. It was to witness how Ted would react to finding a prostitute waiting for him in the room. The girl had thoughtfully been booked by Sid. Ted recalls: "She thought the prank was hilarious, particularly with the entire company let in on it. We all had a good laugh. My comment to the girl was: 'Sorry, I'm broke

– and secondly I'm taken!' Giggling, she headed off to Sid's dressing room… to collect her fee, of course." What a carry on…

Ted was particularly amused by Lou Herbert, the big, tough actor who played Big Julie. At one point during the show, Sky has to throw a punch at Big Julie and Ted's 'blow', which deliberately missed the chin, was matched by a slapping noise off stage to add realism. Big Julie would then slump to the floor.

One night, Lou, with his thick Brookyn accent, said: "Hey Ted, hit me, really hit me. I used to be a boxer. I'd love it!" Ted was reluctant and joked that he might want to take up the guitar some day. But as luck would have it that night, for once, Ted accidently misdirected the punch, catching Lou with full impact on the chin. As he slid down, Lou was heard by the two thousand plus audience to mutter…"Dat was beautiful, Ted. Dat was beautiful."

§ § §

CHAPTER

10

Alfred Marks burst in, totally naked and wearing his spectacles in a very unusual place...

Guys and Dolls ran for 18 months and Ted, firmly established as a proven crowd-puller in West End shows, and as a major 'British' entertainer, then added a third lead role to his growing list of appearances in great American musicals. Although the venue – the Coliseum – was the same, the role of Judge Forestier in Can-Can was in total contrast to Billy Bigelow and Sky Masterson. On reading the script and assessing the character of the Judge, Ted felt slightly uneasy about taking the role. This was a far more frivolous and lightweight storyline. The saving grace was the music – by the great Cole Porter – and this influenced Ted greatly in taking the decision to accept the part. The rather serious Judge reminded Ted of some of the French Canadians he had come across in Montreal where his brother Jack was in business.

Indeed, Ted would have played the part with a strong accent to match the genuine Gallic tones of his leading lady, Irene Hilda, a stunning cabaret star in her native France. Oddly, in retrospect, the American producers directed the entire cast to deliver all dialogue in their normal accents, as was the case in the Broadway production. But the audiences did not seem to mind this.

Ted added a distinguished touch to his portrayal of the Judge by growing his first ever moustache, and having his sideburns silvered. With slicked-back hair and immaculate suit he brought every ounce of dignity into his role – then visibly melting as the can-can ignites the inner parts that law school tried to dampen down.

Irene played her part enthusiastically, and the near-carnivorous kissing scenes perhaps indicated the hunger of a girl far from home, and – apart from occasional visits – denied the attention of her husband, who was in Paris. The audience used to cheer lustily to encourage Irene and stoke her passion. Ted, more than happy with the kisses he got at home, says he was unmoved, regarding the need to be in a passionate clinch with a sensuous Parisian chanteuse eight times a week as something he simply had to suffer in the interests of his chosen profession!

The sublime Irene created love interest in Can-Can. Alfred Marks was noteworthy for if not the ridiculous, for a display of broad comedy that some nights took him out of character and into the realms of a one-man cabaret. The audience loved his portrayal as an eccentric artist, and Ted rejoiced in his company as a prankster. But perhaps it was a step too far when Ted, entertaining friends in his dressing room, had an unexpected visit from Alfred (who was used to popping in with his latest joke). Because when he burst through the door, expecting only Ted to be there, he was stark naked except for his glasses which were being worn on his privates, secured by tape. There was no way of making a dignified exit. Fortunately, the visitors were all 'pros' who knew Alfred well!

Ted says: "Alfred was a loveable performer who could be outrageous but who was always fun to be with. I remember one night when he had the misfortune to lose a tooth from the front of his upper dentures. He had a lot of laughing to do during the show and was feeling terrible because he was very conscious of the huge gap up front. As a gag, Warren Mitchell (in his first major role) and I arrived on stage for one scene – and we'd each blacked out a tooth with make-up. He took one look at us and blew up completely. The scene was supposed to be his, with us reacting to him, but his dialogue was reduced to choking, spluttering mayhem. What the audience made of it I'll never know!"

Ted felt that the great strength of Can-Can was the dancing, though those memorable Cole Porter songs, *C'est Magnifique* and *I Love Paris*, became standards and Ted recorded both and used them in concert and cabaret for many years to come. Leading the dancing was Gillian Lynne who went on to become an incomparable choreographer and who was still in demand half a century after her dancing in Can-Can provided a feast for the eye.

Ted saw quite a lot of her… in the most literal sense! "I remember her perfect dancer's figure and her immense talent. But I also remember that she had one strange habit. She refused to wear a stitch of clothing in her dressing room when cooling off between scenes. If you walked in on her, there she was, starkers. But there was never a trace of a blush. You could take it or leave it."

During the run of Can-Can, Ted, always looking for a new hobby to pursue, really got into painting as a way of relaxing. It was just one of a wide range of enthusiasms adopted – or in some cases revived from his Canadian boyhood – to relax and fill in time before shows. A wad of newspaper cuttings from the time, of interviews Ted gave in towns and cities, illustrates the point – there are pictures of him sailing, fishing, swimming, taking photographs, firing a bow, manning a catamaran and with the wind in his hair riding out the waves in a speedboat. One writer, noting Ted had an appetite for new skills and new knowledge, observed: "He can find lots of interest in the place he happens to be at the moment."

§ § §

It was while he was in Can-Can that Terence Cuneo – a famous artist who became a frequent painter of the Royals, as well as of steam trains and war scenes – called at Ted's dressing room and a 40-year friendship was forged. He had been cajoled by his daughter into going to the stage door to ask for Ted's autograph. The professional painter and the amateur enthusiast, whose childhood pencil sketch of a leaping deer had led his mother to encourage him to draw, were soon engrossed in conversation.

They swapped tales of their roles at the Coronation which Ted had experienced in the choir loft and Terence had seen and recorded in a three-hour sketching session from a perch up in the top of the Abbey.

It was a meeting of like-minded men, and of mutual admiration for the talents each had. Terence loved music, Ted loved art, and both loved nature. Ted and Jackie were invited to Terence's home, with studio attached, near Hampton Court. Later they enjoyed days out at the Imperial War Museum site at Duxford, where they both enthused over the warplanes, many of which Terence had depicted in his military paintings.

One subject Ted the painter had tackled was a racehorse owned by another visitor to the dressing room, a fabulously wealthy South African gold mine owner called Jack Gerber. Between shows, Ted produced a portrait of one of his horses which had won the Stewards' Cup at Goodwood – a picture that Terence Cuneo described as 'an equestrian work of some merit'. Jack and Ted, a lover of horse racing, also became great friends. He would sometimes watch the show from the wings and then visit Ted's dressing room for drinks, as one of a string of regular visitors, who included Errol Flynn.

Most visitors were warmly welcomed but there was another caller who was making himself a nuisance – and who was found to be dropping in when Ted was not there to sample the drinks he kept for people being brought backstage.

The situation was getting out of hand and a member of the staff, all of whom were aware of the identity of the culprit, whispered to Ted: "Get a hamster. He can't stand small pets of any kind." So Ted bought 'Billy Bigelow' and he was installed in a little cabin built by the stage carpenters. The result, when the 'gentleman' next visited, was instant and dramatically effective. As he came in to the room, he took one look at 'Billy' and froze, before spinning round and heading for the door. In his rush to flee he forgot the two steps at the dressing room door and, catching his toe on the top step, crashed across the corridor and slammed against Irene Hilda's door, coming to rest half in and half out of her room.

Needless to saw, the phantom freeloader never darkened Ted's door again.

§ § §

With the sexy Irene Hilda in a sizzling scene from Can Can at the London Coliseum

Jack Gerber, the South African gold mine owner, and my painting of his horse. I found painting in my dressing room very relaxing.

The guardian of my dressing room, 'Billy Bigelow' the hamster.

A new role and a new hair cut! Here I am as Sid Sorokin in Pajama Game

Above: A special trip home during a break from Pajama Game. For the first time in seven years I met the family – mum and dad, both 80, and my brothers (from the left) Ralph, Murray and Jack.

Right: Having fun in Pajama Game with Joy Nichols, Liz Seal and Max Wall.

Partnering Vanessa Leigh in a scene from Oklahoma! for BBC TV.

On set with fellow Canadian and friend from the war years Robert Farnon, the great composer, conductor and arranger.

CHAPTER
11

"It was like an imaginary shepherd's crook, yanking Joan through the air and off!"

By the Autumn of 1955 Ted Hockridge had spent five years taking to the stage night after night in West End musicals. He had also done dozens of radio broadcasts, ranging from appearances on the Commonwealth of Song series, to Workers' Playtime, to Henry Hall's Guest Night spots, and an increasing number of TV bookings.

He was building up a huge fan base and his name was familiar to anyone enjoying popular music. One journalist referred to him as being the 'resident lead' in West End shows. The question was: What comes next? It was prompted by the news that Can-Can would be coming off soon – after an 18-month run. But that news was accompanied by an intriguing post-script: Pajama Game, then running on Broadway, would be taking its place. Ted had received the LP of the show from a friend in America and loved what he heard.

At first it was rumoured that John Raitt would come over from Broadway to continue in the role of Sid Sorokin but that proved to be unfounded. There was a wonderful opening there for someone but with the tendency of American producers to be inflexible over their choice of leads, that person would probably have to be a Raitt look-alike.

As Can-Can wound down, auditions started for the incoming show, which had lyrics by Dick Adler and music by Jerry Ross. Behind the scenes, the production people had been doing their homework and, of course, knew of Ted's success in major London productions that had all been hits. They liked his credentials but they were looking for an all-American pajama factory manager and at that moment, Ted, or rather Forestier, with his slicked back hair, debonair sideburns, and pencil moustache, was a far cry from the character they had in mind! It was time to be proactive, Ted decided. As soon as he was able to cast aside his role as the Judge, he went in search of a look that might convince the Pajama Game people that he was a Sid in the making. He told his barber: "Right. Off with the moustache, off with the sideburns – and give me a one-and-a-half inch GI style haircut!"

The finished effect was not far removed from the way Raitt had looked on Broadway, and although Jackie's eyes nearly popped out of her head at the transformation, and the BBC started to wonder about a wig for future singing appearances, the American producers Ted met seemed to approve. But no decision could be taken without the approval of Adler and Ross, who with Guys and Dolls and Damn Yankees behind them were regarded as the great white hopes of the world of musicals. Sadly, Jerry Ross became seriously ill and had been flown home (he was to die within weeks). In the end, confirmation had to come from Dick. It was a long time coming.

Ted waited patiently. Then the phone rang. It was Hal Prince, the producer of the show, inviting Edmund over to his hotel suite in Park Lane. He went through the script with Ted and they walked and talked through the scenes together. Then he asked Ted to sing the score through to him once more. Finally he slowly turned round, looked Ted in the eye and said: "It's yours, kid!"

§ § §

Ted felt that the role of Sid Sorokin was fairly straightforward – and he loved the music… *Hey There, Hernando's Hideaway, A New Town Is A Blue Town, There Once Was A Man.* Hey There was to be a hit of the show, and a personal triumph for Ted. The production company had decided to bring out an LP just after Pajama Game had opened but then opted to do it just before the opening, one consideration being that a disc could be flown to Jerry in New York for him to hear as he lay dying. Ted remembers: "The entire company and orchestra were all fired up with the desire to show Jerry how proud we were of his work and thrilled to be performing it in London. We started at ten in the morning in the HMV Abbey Road studios and by eight at night we had the entire show in the can.

"This was unprecedented. After all, the show hadn't opened yet and although we knew in our hearts that it would be a success, it might have flopped. It was an amazing feat of recording – after all, pop groups take weeks and sometimes months to complete an LP. As it happened the show and the LP were very successful but most importantly, Jerry was able to listen to the LP over and over again before his death."

In the show, Hey There was sung by Ted as a duet with himself. For the first time in a musical, a tape recorder was used to enable Ted to respond on stage to his own taped singing, with comments, and then to harmonise in a chorus with his own voice. The number was lifted from the LP and was soon being played regularly on radio, and noticed by the music press. As the disc climbed the charts, the Record Mirror said: "It's a melody that sticks in the brain. I shudder to think how many records there will be of it out there…"

This gave a big boost to Ted's recording career. *Young And Foolish, Sixteen Tons* and *No Other Love* took Ted into the Top 20. Ironically for a Canadian, records were placed high up in several successive charts showing Biggest Sales by British Artists! For several years afterwards he would be recording regularly, cutting more than 250 tracks in all.

When EMI held a big party for its stars, Ted was on a guest list that was a billboard of the popular recording artists of the day – Alma Cogan, Kathy Kay, Norrie Paramour, Max Jaffa, Bert Weedon, Victor Silvester and Michael Holliday were in the listing.

Throughout his life, Ted has been associated with sheer singing power. Mention his name and many will say, "Oh yes, the Canadian with the big voice". But many of his recordings in the Fifties, and later, showed his ability to find the lighter and more tender tones when the song demanded it. When he began to be regarded as a Top 20 star, the Record Mirror took pains to praise this flexibility which equipped him to sing romantic ballads and a host of songs that called for an intimate treatment: "He's no blaster. He can pull down his voice to a whisper with the ease of someone turning a volume control."

Hey There and the releases that came shortly afterwards helped to extend Ted's following among younger people. Their support for *No Other Love* projected it to a Top 20 spot and for a time it was well above Elvis's *Heartbreak Hotel* and Bill Haley's *See You Later Alligator*. His appearance on a TV pop show with his new GI haircut for Pajama Game came as a complete surprise to his fans.

Recording songs and being a 'celebrity' were satisfying diversions from Ted's main business in Pajama Game which continued to bring in the crowds and which had received royal approval; the Queen Mother and Princess Margaret came several times to see it.

Ted found his leading lady Joy Nichols easy to work with and he was full of admiration for the dancing of Elizabeth Seal, whose performances became a highlight of the musical. He also found delight in being in the company of Max Wall, although Max's endless trumpet-playing in the next-door dressing room was enough to test any friendship. "Max was so unpredictable and always a load of laughs", says Ted. "The whole company understood his eccentricities, admired his brilliance and adored him."

One night Ted and Max were involved in a little unscripted drama when another member of the cast, Joan Emney (sister of Fred), a large and jovial middle-aged lady appeared a little more uninhibited than usual as she took to the stage for her nightly song and dance number with Max. In fact she had just returned from a wedding reception where, evidently, the wine had been very good and this showed in her dancing. It was so frenetic that Max feared decapitation or worse and scrambled upstage to avoid flying limbs.

The stage manager's voice boomed over the intercom, demanding that the understudy be rushed down immediately. Max then managed to manoeuvre Joan close to the wings, and a pair of hands flashed out just long enough to yank Joan off… and for the identically-dressed understudy to pick up the routine. Ted recalls: "It was as if there was an imaginary shepherd's crook around Joan's neck, yanking her through the air, cartoon-style!"

One of the minor characters in Pajama Game, playing a pyjama salesman, was Arthur Lowe, a quiet, unassuming actor of obvious talent, although at the time no-one could have foreseen the great success that awaited him. He and Ted became good friends during the run and 25 years later they were reunited briefly when Ted was doing a summer season and Arthur a play in an adjacent theatre.

By that time Arthur had found his niche as the unforgettable Captain Mainwaring, of Dad's Army, one of the greatest and most durable comic characters to come out of British television. When they met again that summer, Ted and Arthur spent some good times together and were reminded vividly of their Pajama Game days when they visited a local college to see students rehearsing for their own production of the show.

§ § §

Ted had not seen his family in Canada for 10 years. As his father's 80th birthday approached, and there was talk of a celebration reunion, he asked the management if he could be released for a week or so to fly to Vancouver. They agreed to Neville Whiting, Ted's understudy, stepping in.

When the Canadian Broadcasting Corporation heard that Ted would be back in Canada they asked him to appear in a TV spectacular show, the General Electric Hour, they were staging. Spectacular was the word; everything – sets, stage, orchestra and the size of the audience – was on a massive scale, and they had lined up some of the biggest names in entertainment, including the Dave Brubeck Quartet, the young Eartha Kitt and Shirley Jones, who had just starred with Gordon Macrae in Hollywood versions of Oklahoma! and Carousel.

Ted and Shirley performed a selection from Carousel, the musical that meant so much to both of them. It included the duet *If I Loved You,* the *Soliloquy* and the great chorus number *Never Walk Alone.* Ted was unaware that show was being filmed – and 45 years later an ecstatic niece rang from Vancouver to say that she had just seen her uncle in a repeat of the production on TV.

The journey home started pleasantly enough but then turned into drama. The flight crew of the Lockheed Constellation were all Royal Canadian Air Force veterans and they invited him on to the flight deck for the Atlantic crossing.

Ted remembers: "There was a lot of laughter and good-natured reminiscence going on when at 21,000 feet the port outer engine suddenly burst into flames. Activation of the fire extinguisher built into the engine, and a dive down to 5,000 feet, making the plane slide to starboard to blow the flames outwards, did the trick. Calls were sent everywhere, to Gander, Iceland, Shannon, Atlantic shipping, air sea rescue establishing our position. We pressed on with three engines – and with our fingers crossed! – and after a few hours an RAF Shackleton arrived alongside and escorted us to Heathrow. When I finally reached the Coliseum for that evening's performance of Pajama Game Jackie told me she had not slept well all night, as the drama was going on, feeling that there was something wrong."

Ted's new home had become London, although he was not yet free to marry Jackie, who, with Terry, commuted each day from Brighton – bringing their dogs with them. Terry's pooch, a mongrel, was called Pidge and Jackie had a standard poodle, Beau Geste.

A rail strike prevented their daily journeys for a time and they installed themselves in the top-most flat of a four-storey building above the 2 Is coffee bar, in Soho, where Tommy Steele had been discovered. Living beneath them, one on each floor, were three ladies of the night, each with a French name, a personal maid and at least one of them with a poodle. You can only guess how the professional life of Jackie and Terry, given their co-tenants, might have been misunderstood – especially as a virile-looking Ted would regularly make flying visits to 'the establishment' at lunch-time, or on his way to and from the theatre, to call in on the two girls.

Dickie Henderson was quick to spot the construction that could have been put on Ted's visits, remarking: "In my time I've been called West End Willie but you, Ted, must be known as The Iron Man of Soho!"

§ § §

Early days in my recording career. Over the years I recorded 250 tracks for Pye, HMV and Decca.

Jackie when we were in Pajama Game together.

The Taylor Maids – Jackie on the left and Terry, now Mrs Barry Cryer

CHAPTER
12

"It's sand and sea...
happy days,
happy nights making love"

Ted now had a greater peace of mind about Eileen. He had bought a farm in Devon and had stocked it with a herd of Guernsey heifers, and a cattle breeding programme was started. Eileen, who now had a man in her life, had gone to live there and staff were brought in to manage it.

Jackie and Terry moved from the Soho flat to one in Westbourne Terrace and Ted moved in to live with them. Terry and Ted were like sister and brother. Ted never had a sister, and Terry lost her only brother in an RAF air crash. As Ted put it, "I guess a man sharing a flat with two lovely girls in those days must have raised a few eyebrows. But our consciences were clear, and anyway, we just didn't give a damn! Mind you, nowadays, we may have made a few front page headlines."

It was 1957 and Pajama Game finished its successful run of 18 months, in March. There was no other immediate opening in West End musicals for Ted, who had created a record run of leading roles – four in succession over a period of seven years – and 'lived' in the same dressing room for around five of those years! American musicals were certainly the big thing in Britain now, and Ted wondered what his next role would be – and whether it would be in a musical. Would there be a fifth consecutive hit for him in the West End? The solution came when Lillian Aza became his agent.

During the war years Lillian did a great favour for three brothers, a song and dance act in variety, named Leslie, Lou and Bernard. The brothers had started a theatrical agency, which Lillian handled for them while they did their military service, and this was something they never forgot. Under her guidance, work from the rapidly-growing agency of Leslie Grade and Bernard Delfont began to pour in for Ted.

Ted was on the edge of a new phase of his career, a life full of variety (quite literally sometimes!) yet with a routine that tended to follow a set pattern – TV shows, summer seasons, followed by pantomime in the winter. Recordings, cabaret, concert appearances and broadcasts slotted in along the way. The new challenge for him was to communicate with the audience, without being able to hide behind a theatrical character in costume. Suddenly, there were no cues, and no plot.

Looks can deceive, and it is likely that behind what has always appeared to be a cool, laid-back and confident stage presence, lay a much more reserved and even shy performer – a contradiction hinted at in earlier press 'crits', which suggested that there was a degree of seriousness behind Ted's stage persona. Jackie believes that behind Ted's full-on interplay with the audience was indeed a measure of shyness, coupled with a touch of nerves that all true performers need to feel to give their best. He was quick to adapt, however, and from his first summer season – at the Theatre Royal, Bournemouth, with Saveen on the bill, and Jackie as principal dancer – he gained experience and confidence in this entirely new field, so different from musicals.

In his own words, he was now "ready for anything" – and anything, and everything, followed rapidly. Within a year he sang in 35 concerts all over Britain, including one at the Festival Hall, hosted ITV Saturday Spectaculars, made appearances on Sunday Night At The London Palladium, appeared on 26 BBC shows (TV and radio) and starred in numerous cabaret venues, including the Dorchester and Grosvenor House hotels in Park Lane. Somehow or other he also fitted in 15 weeks of variety touring!

The early years of singing on radio and then in musicals had laid the foundations for the popularity he enjoyed in his new ventures. His fame went before him, and he found that the audiences he was reaching needed no convincing; it was common for fans to approach him with the words "I remember hearing you…" or "I'll never forget seeing you in…" He also had the support of the musical director Jimmy Bailey, who had been with the legendary Gracie Fields for some years. Through Jimmy, Gracie became great friends with Ted and Jackie.

In the autumn, Ted was booked to do a variety tour and in Peterborough he appeared with Bill Maynard. For this date, Ted and Bill – along with the rest of the cast – were puzzled as to why, instead of the usual juggler, conjurer or dancers opening the show, a young and inexperienced pop band started off the evening. The local management were not impressed but how wrong they were. The group's name was …The Beatles!

§ § §

In the new year, before Ted's first summer season at the North Pier, Blackpool, Ted and Jackie decided to take a much-needed break. So for a while work was forgotten and in Spring they flew the car from Lydd Airport in Kent to Le Touquet and headed south. Jackie had not passed her test and so Ted did all the driving, clocking 600 miles through the night. They snatched meals and naps on the way and, arriving at dawn, before their hotel had opened, slept on the beach at Le Rayole. Settling in, they found that the hotel owner was a theatrical man who had been on the stage in Montmatre in the Twenties, working with Maurice Chevalier.

The couple had an unforgettably happy time together. Later in his career, Ted recorded an album called International Songs For International Lovers and a line from one of the songs, *Sand and Sea*, summed up their holiday… "happy days, happy nights, making love." The song was to have extra meaning later when their first-born son, Murray, as a toddler, would listen to the LP and sing along with it (one day, after the words 'making love' he added his own observation: "Mummy makes pies!").

The North Pier show turned out to be a tremendous success. This was a real spectacular, produced and choreographed by Ernest Maxim, who was in great demand in TV. Ted immediately hit it off with Billy Dainty and David Nixon, and also met Joan Regan for the first time, a significant moment, as was Ted's meeting with a Paul Burnett, a musician from Yorkshire. Paul was a keyboard player with great ability with orchestrations. After joining the Delfont organisation he was installed as resident conductor at the Prince of Wales Theatre, London and some years later became Ted's musical director. When during that summer in Blackpool Paul married Sally, a dancer and singer, Ted was his best man, and they became lifelong friends.

The banter that went on in the theatre between David Nixon, Billy Dainty and Ted was legendary. One day, David Nixon decided to try to learn to water ski in the Lake District, and broke his ankle in the process. Because he was on crutches he had to take a ride in a wheelchair every day down to the theatre, which was at the end of the pier. He was a bit embarrassed about this and, trying to hide his identity, wore a false beard and sunglasses.

Before one show, Ted and Billy, who had borrowed a megaphone, stood on the roof of the theatre announcing to members of the audience walking up the pier to the show: "Ladies and gentlemen…The person in the wheelchair with a beard is…David Nixon! He would be only too pleased to say hello and sign autographs for you. " All eyes turned on the unfortunate magic man who wished at the time he could have made himself disappear.

That year – 1958 – also saw a dramatic change in Jackie's career. While Ted had been in Guys and Dolls and Can-Can, during the previous year, she had appeared at The Hippodrome, Leicester Square, in A Wedding in Paris with Anton Walbrook and Evelyn Laye (Jackie found 'Boo' Laye to be a real lady and totally unaffected despite her standing in musical theatre). Then Jackie joined the cast of The Bells Are Ringing at the Coliseum, and she and Terry decided to form a double act, The Taylor Maids, a glamorous duo, wearing stunning gowns and singing popular music, with some dancing.

Ted's agent, Lillian Aza, had immediately taken them under her wing and they were soon on their way to becoming known nationally, doing TV appearances on the Joan Regan Show, New Faces and then on the Tommy Trinder show, Trinder Box which led to The Taylor Maids being invited to appear as a duo in panto, with Jackie playing Dandini and Terry Principal Boy. There were also variety tours with the Billy Cotton Band Show.

As Ted began his summer season at Blackpool, Lillian Aza secured a plum booking for the Taylor Maids – a once-a-week TV variety show called Holiday Town Parade, starring such notables as Joe Loss and his band and McDonald Hobley, as compere. The show went to a different seaside resort each Saturday – and by an incredible coincidence all of the venues were down the North West coast, so Ted and Jackie could stay together. They rented a house for the season and Terry joined them. Ted says: "We were probably the talk of the town, especially as three more men joined them as guests! The King Brothers, who were also at the North Pier, had dreadful digs and Jackie, feeling sorry for them, took them in until they found their own new accommodation. They were nice guys and we all had a good laugh."

Ted followed his first summer season at Blackpool with a no-expense-spared London Palladium panto production of The Sleeping Beauty, joining Bruce Forsyth, Charlie Drake and Bernard Breslaw.

After the opening night of what was a prestigious show, Ted and Jackie joined Bruce and his first wife Penny, for supper at The Pigalle Club. Diane Coral, who, like Penny, was a dancer, and her husband Bernard, also came along to see Sammy Davis Jnr in cabaret . Then someone suggested that they go down to Fleet Street to get the newspapers hot off the press and read the 'crits' of the show. While they waited, late at night, for the first editions, they struck up as a glee club, singing carols in the street –being joined by the printing staff as they came off shift. A night to remember – and the 'crits' turned out to be great too!

To ensure that the sets of the show looked suitably splendid, Robert Nesbit, who as a legend of stage lighting was known rather grandly – and with an element of contradiction – as The Prince of Darkness, had been brought from Las Vegas to oversee the production. He was treated with great deference by all, everyone calling him "Mr Nesbit", except Ted who saw no reason to call him anything but Bob ("Typically Canadian!" says Ted).

There was a Western scene during which Ted's horse, Winston, a circus pony, would clatter on stage, coming to a halt at the last minute on the brink of the orchestra pit, terrifying the musicians. One night, Winston decided to leave, on stage, a steaming memento of his appearance, and Charlie Drake had the cast in hysterics when, spotting it, he fixed it with a stare and shouted: "Don't touch it anyone – Mr Nesbit hasn't lit it yet!"

There was great hilarity on another night when Dorothy Dampier, a wonderfully weird witch, lost much of her menace and composure when she got stuck half way down a trap door that jammed, so that only half of her disappeared. Soon afterwards another little disaster befell her. During each performance she would fly off into the wings on a wire, and when she was out of sight of the audience, would be caught by one of the stagehands on a high platform in the flies. He would help her down safely. Unfortunately, one night the magic turned to mayhem as he fumbled the catch… and poor Dorothy re-appeared on stage, swinging backwards and forwards pleading: "Get me down, get me down!"

Ted also became a victim of thespian gremlins. He played the handsome prince and, in a dramatic moment during the show, was challenged to show his expertise with his shotgun, as gipsies around the camp fire watched expectantly. When he fired high above the stage, a dove – out of sight above the audience – would fall as if from the sky. There was a fail safe arrangement: if the dove didn't fall, a stage hand called George would throw one from the wings, high enough for it to drop down realistically onto the centre stage and, hopefully save the scene.

During one performance, George was off with flu and another man, Fred, was supposed to do the business. Ted fired his first shot, but nothing fell. Knowing that another dove would be thrown into the air, to land convincingly from the 'sky' (it was hoped), he fired his second shot. Again there was no dove. Then the whole theatre heard the stage manager shouting: "For God's sake throw it!"

Fred threw it all right, but not high in the air; he chose to send it sliding across the stage and through Ted's legs! The cast and the audience fell about laughing and things went from bad to worse when someone, in the general panic, leaned on the fire sprinkler button and set it going!

In the following May, Ted and Jackie planned another holiday in France before a second season in Blackpool. This time, before they left, Jackie secretly took some driving lessons. Her test was on the Monday before their scheduled departure on the Wednesday. Jackie says, "Thankfully I passed it first time, but my first driving after my lessons was done on the wrong side of the road. I think I scared Ted to death at times but we made it!"

After four days of sun, the Mistral (that chilling wind off the Alps) arrived. They left the coast and drove hundreds of miles, up into the mountains of France and Switzerland, loving every minute of it. Arriving in Switzerland they booked into a hotel near Interlaken, a room with a beautiful view overlooking Lake Thun and the mountains – very romantic! But that night they were brought down to earth...when they met a party of holidaymakers from Worthing, where Ted had just done a concert before starting the holiday. C'est la vie...

Ted was the first featured star ever to have had his contract renewed by the North Pier management for a consecutive season. It was a great compliment. And because the Taylor Maids were also doing a second season with Holiday Town Parade, they rented a house again. For this new season, Harry Worth starred alongside Ted and again Billy Dainty was on the bill. As before, the chemistry worked and they had a great show.

Ted and Harry, along with Billy, would sometimes try to fit in a game of golf. On one occasion Harry finished putting and absent-mindedly put the putter in the hole and the flag in his bag. Ted said: "Billy and I pretended not to notice. But unfortunately for Harry some well-meaning, good-natured fans who were also golfing, and waiting at a nearby tee, witnessed all and cracked up laughing. No doubt they were thinking that this was par for the course for Harry!"

The summer seasons were hard work. As well as doing two shows a night, Ted would also have to fit in Sunday concerts within reach of Blackpool but often considerable distances away, in places such as Scarborough (this was before we had motorways). However he and Jackie grabbed what leisure time they could and explored the countryside south of the Lake District in the Forest of Boland.

Now that Ted was in a cycle of summer shows, pantomime and variety, the world of musicals seemed an age away. But the arrival of an unexpected invitation took him right back to Carousel and into the company of the two men who wrote it, Richard Rodgers and Oscar Hammerstein. Along with Dame Sybil Thorndike and her husband, Sir Lewis Casson, Ted was invited as a guest to the annual dinner of the First Nighters Club. Although he was unaware of it, the two greats of the modern musical – in London for a few days in connection with the forthcoming production of The Sound Of Music – were also guests.

Ted remembers: "There were some excellent speeches and tributes to actors and actresses and of course to the supreme guests, Rodgers and Hammerstein. Then someone got a bright idea: 'Why not get the man who played Billy Bigelow in the London production of Carousel up to do a song from the show'. But what was in mind was not just any song but the Soliloquy, as a tribute to the distinguished pair."

Ted said: "My first thought was the old opera adage 'Never sing on a full stomach'! My second was that I hadn't done the Soliloquy for ages. Would I remember it? My third thought: Who'll accompany me? And finally… how was I going to put over, with conviction, the seven emotion-packed minutes of in-depth lyrics on the problems of forthcoming fatherhood, standing there in my dinner suit? A London theatre conductor who knew the music stepped in and so I was trapped. I was petrified for a moment but just as in battle there's no turning back when you go over the top. I soldiered on. Without a moment's rehearsal, my conductor friend (who was familiar with the music but not my interpretation) and I plunged into our off-the-cuff rendition.

"I assumed from their generous applause that Rodgers and Hammerstein had enjoyed it. At the end of the evening, as we shook hands, Oscar said: 'A most extraordinary interpretation. Quite different from any I have heard before. It set me thinking about my lyrics… even so we enjoyed it immensely' he added with a wicked grin".

In the autumn of that year, 1959, the Blackpool season was followed by a seven-week autumn run in Coventry. With TV still in its infancy and theatre still enjoying its heyday staging musicals, Coventry's Spring Show and the autumn Birthday Show were top dates.

With Ted that year in the Birthday Show were Arthur Haynes and Freddie Frinton, both seasoned performers who were now beginning to make their mark on television.

Ted remembers that Arthur was an insomniac and would play anyone at poker. Freddie was a regular and although Ted joined him and Freddie, a regular, for a couple of sessions he soon began to excuse himself. "Late nights are no good for the singing voice" Ted says. "Arthur died young and I'm sure those late nights and early mornings did not help."

For the pantomime that Christmas, Humpty Dumpty at Southampton, Ted joined Petula Clark and Tommy Cooper on the bill. He said: "It was the first time I had worked with Tommy and it was a laugh from start to finish. I'd done TV with Pet and it was always a pleasure as she was a very professional gal to work with, but this was our first stage show together." It was during this pantomime run (while doing a TV show in France on a Sunday break) that she met her French husband-to-be. While in the show, Ted learned of an amusing show business myth that seemed to be circulating. It had been picked up by Petula, who related it with delight to Jackie.

Pet had been in a hairdressers, and while she in the chair, Ted's name was mentioned. "Oooh," said the hairdresser, "he's gorgeous," reflecting a popular view among women at the time.

Then she added: "Pity he's queer…"

§ § §

Three pictures of me as the Prince in Sleeping Beauty at the Palladium. Left, with cast members Charlie Drake and Bernard Breslaw. And above on a circus pony called Winston whose arrival each night scared the hell out of the cast. Incidentally in this very successful show Bruce Forsyth was the court jester.

Harry Worth protests that he was only joking when he put the golf flag in his bag and his club in the hole. The picture was taken in Blackpool.

Billy Dainty and Harry Worth – a great pair to work with.

CHAPTER

13

"We went for a walk and Ted said: 'I've just had a call from Eileen. The divorce can go ahead.'"

It was 1960, a momentous year for Ted and Jackie, a year that marked the sweeping away of what had been and the beginning of what they had waited for during nine long years.

The year started dramatically enough, with Ted having to seek treatment for a problem that was impairing his voice. Like all singers, he lived in fear of colds and infections and, increasingly, he was having sinus trouble. It was time to seek the advice of J. Ivor Griffiths, a pioneering ear, nose and throat specialist, who had helped singers from all over the world – including world famous opera stars from La Scala, Milan – to keep their vocal equipment in good shape as well as maharajahs with throat problems. In fact, years before, he had extended Ted's singing career by imploring him to stop smoking, and telling him how to do it.

Ted was in Guys and Dolls at the time and when he encountered a problem with his voice, he heard from Evelyn Laye about this remarkable specialist who had helped Jack Hawkins to speak again after his throat operation. He had questioned Ted about his smoking that dated back to his days in the Royal Canadian Air Force, when cigarettes were issued free. Griffiths had seen Ted in Carousel and remarked that, although the singing had been wonderful, Ted could not expect to produce those sort of performances unless he stopped smoking immediately. In fact, he predicted that within five years Ted would not be singing at all.

He outlined a technique to ease Ted off nicotine, drawing up a plan, which involved Ted having his first cigarette of the day later and later. This would continue until he was smoking only the two cigarettes he had during Guys and Dolls. When the show ended, Ted would be a non-smoker. Ted remembers; "There was one scene in the show that I looked forward to, because it was my chance for that cigarette. In the script it was five o'clock in the morning on Broadway and I would lean against a lamp-post, light a cigarette and sing *My Time of Day*. I spun the cigarette out so long that the poor conductor would often have his baton raised, waiting until I got a fleeting nicotine fix! By the end of the run, I had weaned myself off the weed."

As the new year started, Ted's sinus trouble was proving a problem and he revisited Griffiths, who agreed to undertake what was then his pioneering operation which would mean that sinus blockages would be a thing of the past. In the same week he operated on a very promising opera singer whose career was also suffering – Joan Sutherland. Both operations were successful, and both careers took off to new heights (Joan, of course, became a singer of world renown). Ivor always said that Joan and Edmund were his favourite guinea pigs; and understandably, as far as they were concerned, he was the greatest.

Later Ted and Jackie went on tour, Ted the singing star on the bill and Jackie appearing with Terry in the Taylor Maids, who were enjoying growing success. While enjoying a walk alongside the river at Wetherby, in Yorkshire, Ted turned to Jackie and said: "I've just had a call from Eileen. The divorce can go ahead." Eileen was going to get married, Ian was well into his teens and so, at long last a line could be drawn under their marriage.

Despite her happiness at hearing this news after such a long wait, the passing of time had, for Jackie, made matters much less straightforward than they would have been if Ted had been free to marry soon after they had met. In fact, there were difficult decisions to be made, and these tempered Jackie's joy at hearing the good news.

With a cruel irony, Jackie was enjoying building a career with Terry and there was now every indication that the future was very bright for the song-and-dance duo. They had behind them a string of high-profile appearances, they had sung in front of some great bands, such as Joe Loss and Billy Cotton, and had done cabaret tours abroad. They had also caught the nation's eye on the TV show New Faces.

Their appearances on the talent show, and on Holiday Town Parade, sparked a flurry of fan letters, some from men, who evidently were set drooling over the leggy pair, and some from young girls wanted to know how to become glamorous dancers. One particularly idolatrous letter, from an officer in the Admiralty Constabulary, seemed to sum up the appeal of the Taylor Maids – singing talent ("so much better than some of the squawking we get on TV"), dancing talent ("the Television Toppers aren't a patch on you"), and jaw-dropping beauty.

The considered verdict of Constable Needham and his fellow officers was that the Taylor Maids were "the ideal pin-up figures." Obviously still transfixed by the TV routine he had ogled over, he added: "If we are not sticking our necks out too far, ladies, could you oblige the Station with a photo similar to that part of the act after you discarded your long skirts and started to dance."

Just before Ted had received the phone call from Eileen, Jackie and Terry had spent a considerable amount of money on musical arrangements and gowns but now the future was in doubt. After all, Jackie was 28 and if she and Ted were going to marry and have a family, they would not have to leave it too long. As Ted was in great demand all over the country, could they sustain a marriage if Jackie had Taylor Maids bookings to fulfil here and abroad? There was also Terry to consider. From the earliest dance-class days back in Brighton, through early auditions and then in shows – Bless the Bride, Carousel, Wedding in Paris, Wonderful Town and Pajama Game, and panto with Tommy Trinder – they had been shoulder to shoulder, as they were in the Taylor Maids. What would Terry do if the duo split up?

Jackie says: "I had such mixed emotions when Ted gave me the news. We had waited nine years, and over that time, I sometimes thought that it wasn't going to happen. Sometimes there were terrible doldrums and I had found working very therapeutic. If I was to marry, the act would have to be broken up and I was very worried about Terry."

The deciding factor was the couple's desire to be together and have children. And as it turned out, Jackie's feelings of guilt were eased by a happy outcome for Terry.

Jackie and Ted said that Terry could have the use of their flat for as long as she wanted, particularly as they would be on tour a lot of the time. Later that year, Terry got the role of principal boy in pantomime in Nottingham and met Danny La Rue, who worked at Winston's night club, off Bond Street, in London. He asked her to join him and there she met a young comedian and comedy writer called Barry Cryer whom she later married.

§ § §

To finalise things with Eileen, Ted signed the farm and the herd of Guernseys over to her in settlement . Any worries about the effects on Ian of newspaper reports about the divorce were alleviated by the fact that the press was fully occupied with Aneurin Bevan's death on the day that the divorce went through.

But there was bad news from Canada for Ted while he was appearing in the Palladium summer season. Just before going on stage for a matinee, his brother Murray phoned from Vancouver to say that Dad had died suddenly while watching a football match on TV. Ted went on and carried off his appearance perfectly but in the evening the delayed shock hit him and having to perform was a nightmare. He had always loved and admired his father from the days when they worked together on the farm, and his death was a body blow.

That summer Ted was invited with some of the other biggest names in show business, to take part in a charity show, which had been drawn together with Laurence Olivier as compere. On the afternoon of the show, as rehearsals were going on, Ted sat beside the producer and noticed another man seated at the other side. It suddenly struck him that it was Noel Coward. After a time, Coward asked the producer, "What do you call the show?" The producer replied, "Summer Stars." There was a pause before the incomparable Coward commented languidly, "And summer not."

Ted and Jackie decided to marry towards the end of the summer season. They wanted a low-key affair, and through a family connection, they heard of a wonderful retired missionary who lived in a little Kent village and who officiated at a Baptist church. 'Pop' Taverner agreed to conduct the service and Ted and Jackie accepted the kind invitation of 'Pop' and his wife to stay with them in their home on three occasions, to fulfil the requirements about the pre-wedding banns. It was a cold October, the house had no central heating or hot water and was run on Spartan lines. But they were a charming couple – and, anyway, as Ted and Jackie said later, they had their love to keep them warm.

The wedding was held on Hallowe'en, with only Jackie's mother and two brothers, Ted's former agent Teddy Holmes and a representative of

Pye Records in attendance. No photographer was booked for the sake of privacy but one of Jackie's brothers took some pictures using just the sunlight through the church windows and by happy chance it turned out so well that it was chosen as the cover image for Ted's album *International Songs for International Lovers* some years later. Unfortunately, at the last minute, Terry was unable to share the happy day.

When Ted and Jackie got back to the theatre that night, they made no announcement but told Joan Regan and Billy Dainty. Eventually the news filtered down and a party was held on stage.

The Palladium show had been especially enjoyable. Ted had loved working again with Billy and Joan with whom he shared a nightly giggle over a duet they had to sing. They both wore glasses but took them off for the show, which included a scene where they would have to walk down a staircase together (holding on to each other precariously!) and looking into each other's myopic eyes and singing *I Only Have Eyes for You*.

Joan Regan's dressing room was next to Ted's and as he and Joan's husband were both keen on horse racing, they had a television in each dressing room tuned in to different racing channels. One day, Joan was in her dressing room, interviewing a rather humourless nanny to look after her daughter Donna. Ted was in his boxer shorts getting ready to dress for the next show, when he blithely burst in on Joan to see how the racing was going. Spotting the visitor, he said; "Sorry, I didn't know you had someone here". The suggestiveness of the situation did not raise a smile with the nanny and she was eliminated on the grounds of the lack of a sense of humour.

Russ Conway was also great fun, but he had a habit of being late in arriving and had often broken the unwritten rule that said he should be in the theatre 35 minutes before the start of the show. Russ was given a talking to and Ted and the rest of the cast got together to contrive a jokey way of getting the message across. They bought some meteorological balloons, which were about two foot in diameter when inflated. The stage hands blew these up and, with Russ about to arrive, filled the dressing room to bursting. Russ, late again, opened the door and found he couldn't get in to get dressed. A series of loud bangs was heard as Russ lit a cigarette and blasted his way into the room, and finally managed to get into his stage clothes.

§ § §

The show was a great success and during the summer Pye brought out a 'Joan and Ted' LP. With some personnel changes, it then moved to the Empire Theatre, Glasgow for a winter run, instead of the usual pantomime.

The journey to Glasgow for the Hockridges would be quite taxing, especially as there were no motorways and by that time they had three dogs, Jackie's Beau Geste and two collies, Sheba and Tarn. The idea was to enjoy a meal in their favourite Greek restaurant and try to make Glasgow in one go through the night, so that they would not have to make an overnight stop with the 'family'. In fact, Ted in an estate car with Beau and Jackie driving his Jaguar with the collies in the back, arrived 17 hours later, understandably exhausted.

They had booked a motel in Aberfoyle, to enjoy the countryside, and Billy Dainty and his wife, Sandra, had the adjacent chalet. Because the collies were on heat, Billy had volunteered to keep Beau away from the two bitches. Restless nights followed as the eager pooch tried to get through the wall to the collies.

They had a particularly worrying moment next day, when one of the collies was pursued by an old Highland mongrel up a mountainside. It had been with a couple of Scottish lads. Ted called out to them: "There's half a crown for each of you if you can catch my dog". One of them shouted back reassuringly: "Ye dinna have to worry about him, mister – he's got no teeth." Ted says: "We didn't try to explain that it wasn't his dentures that we were worried about!".

There seemed to be something to smile about at every turn. When Billy and Ted went off golfing in the Trossachs, they found that the greens were immaculate, except for the unexpected layers of sheep droppings preventing a clear putt to any hole.

Ted and Jackie invited Joan and her husband, Harry Claff ,to join them for the weekend, and a mad idea was hatched – to go pony trekking in the snow, in the mountains around Aberfoyle. Ted took a bottle of whisky as a precaution against the cold. Supplying the pony was a hoary old bearded Scot, who appeared to be as tough as old boots. When, frozen through, they each had a nip of whisky, they included the old boy in the 'round'. And although he didn't appear to be feeling the cold, to their horror he virtually polished off the bottle in a series of gulps.

Although the theatre was a 60-mile round trip each day, Ted and Jackie loved the scenery and clean air. They befriended the locals who worked for the Forestry Commission and were allowed to roam mountain trails that reminded Ted of his native Rockies, despite the difference in scale.

Eartha Kitt had joined the show for the Glasgow run and proved a big draw. But she inadvertently misunderstood traditional British protocol on the opening night. In those days casts would commonly sing the national anthem and when, on the final curtain call, they lined up for *God Save The Queen*, Eartha was missing, in her dressing room. Later Ted pointedly, but with good humour, and explained to her that on the next night, if she wanted, she could end the show by singing *The Star Spangled Banner*, but she shouldn't expect the rest of the cast to still be on stage with her!

§ § §

I'm a 'Prince' once again, this time with Tommy Cooper, a great pal and an utterly loveable madman. Playing my Princess was the delightful Petula Clark.

A "last night' party at Torquay with the Mayor, councillors and guests. Tommy is doing his stuff with Ernie Wise at his elbow.

Left: Eartha Kitt and I appeared on the same bill at the Glasgow Empire and helped to pull in the crowds – even if she did not understand our tradition concerning the National Anthem!

Another shot from the Torquay party (I took it on a time switch and managed to squeeze in!). With us are Ernie Wise and Joan Regan.

Left: Billy Dainty, Ron Parry and a very young Des O'Connor ready to perform a sketch in the show at the Glasgow Empire.

Enjoying a London Palladium summer season with co-stars Cliff Richard, Joan Regan and Russ Conway. Also on the bill was Billy Dainty, David Kossoff and young and nervous Des O'Connor.

Terry, Jackie's partner in the Taylor Maids meets Barry Cryer at Winston's nightclub. They worked together there – and fell in love.

A modern setting for my rendition of Largo Al Factotum during the
London Palladium summer season. Cheeky!

There were no professional photographers at our wedding which we kept secret. This lucky shot was taken by Jackie's brother David, using light through a church window. It was later used on the cover of my Decca LP International Songs For International Lovers.

CHAPTER
14

Tommy was in hysterics saying:
"I've got to have
that dog in my act!"

When we look back and reminisce, memories of summers gone by often come to the fore. There's something about long, carefree days in warm weather that makes it the season of good times. For Ted and Jackie the summer of 1961 was an extra special, all they could have hoped for. Although they were now man and wife, they still felt like lovers and they made plans for a belated honeymoon to celebrate the fact that they would now always be together in the future.

Ted was about to start a new summer season in Torquay where Bernard Delfont had signed a contract with the local council to provide productions and artistes for the next five years in the new Princess Theatre, which was just being completed. But first there was a seating problem to sort out with the theatre officials. The problem was the circle. There wasn't one.

Ted and Jackie had travelled down to Torquay to look for accommodation for the season. While there they met Delfont and went with him on a tour of the theatre. Ted recalls that while on stage Delfont looked down at the stalls, which had a capacity for around 1,000 people, and asked: "Where is the circle going?"

The reply was that there was no circle, whereupon Delfont patiently but firmly explained his personal economics policy. "The stalls pay the costs, the circle is my profit. No circle, no shows." Within six weeks there was one, in time for the opening of the theatre.

As soon as the summer run started it was clear that Torquay, 1961, was going to be fun. How could it be anything else with Tommy Cooper looming large and Morecambe and Wise in the ascendency? And the icing on the cake, for Ted and Jackie was that Joan Regan was on the bill.

While Ted and Jackie were down to looking for a house to rent for the season, Ted's weakness for boats of any sort led him to splash out on a fantastic little craft – a Dowty turbo-jet speedboat. As it was jet-driven, there was no need for a propeller and so it could move in only a few inches of water – and it could shift (at 35 knots).

Ted's dressing room had a fire door that gave access to the edge of the harbour where the boat was moored. So on matinee days, between shows, Ted filled the time by hurtling out in the speedboat with fishing tackle at the ready. He'd be back in plenty of time for the evening performance with buckets of mackerel to share with the company.

Ted, Jackie, Joan, Eric and Ernie and Tommy would take it in turns to lay on a party, generally once a week and when it was held on the beach, the Dowty was put to good use for trips out to sea. The Hockridges also found time to go out shark fishing and to sail. The get-togethers gave the funny men in the company a chance to try out their gags in a friendly, informal atmosphere. Ted remembers: "Eric and Ernie were a wonderful audience when they were not making us and everybody else laugh, and they loved Tommy, who was a truly comical and loveable figure.

"Tommy would often test out comic lines that occurred to him. One day he came in with a new joke and, with a bit of conspiring, we all professed to have heard it before. First he went to Ernie and Eric and as he started on the joke they pretended to yawn. He then tried it on us and we did the same. Desperate, he approached Beau, Jackie's dog, and – looking in his eyes – started his story yet again. Bang on cue, Beau yawned too! Tommy was in hysterics, shouting 'I've got to have that dog in my act!' "

One of Tommy Cooper's great assets as a comic was his bulk, and he was often trying to curb his appetite and his weakness for sweets – and for a tipple. With endearing human frailty Caerphilly's most famous son would restrict himself to low-calorie Energen rolls… and then eat everything else as well.

One night, when the town council gave the cast of the show a party, Tommy, who had enjoyed a couple of drinks on the way, found to his chagrin, that his favourite sweet had been on offer, but there was none left for him. To compensate, when Ted and company arranged a private party, as a special treat for Tommy they arranged for the same dessert to be on the menu but by ingenious pre-planning made sure that he was the only one who wasn't served a portion! Tommy immediately twigged and collapsed in laughter.

Eric would sometimes try to get in Tommy's eye-line when he was doing his act, which was already shambolically funny, to try to throw him.

One night it went further and he surprised Tommy – and added a laugh to his act – when, in Tommy's famous hat routine during which he donned various bits of headgear in succession, Tommy put on a hat that Eric had secretly filled with talcum powder!

This was a key time in the development of Morecambe and Wise, who were on the verge of greatness. During the Torquay season they were offered a short-term TV contract and because of a musicians' strike suddenly there was no orchestra or chorus of dancing girls to give the show colour. This panic situation led to a breakthrough in comedy presentation, a winning sketch formula created by Hills and Green, who also featured in the show. This was the launch pad for the classic Morecambe and Wise TV series of future years.

Another winner that summer was Joan Regan. On a day at the steeplechase races with Ted and Jackie she noticed a rank outsider called Big Blunder (and failing to back it turned out to be just that for Ted!). The description on the race card of this nag's paternity explained the unusual name; it said simply 'Sire unknown'. Joan, typically, felt sorry for the horse that didn't know its dad and put her money where her sympathy lay. Ted popped over to the Tote to put her £1 on the 100-1 no-hoper. All the favourites fell, somehow Big Blunder defeated the odds to win – and soon Ted was handing over £100 in fivers to a delighted Joan.

§ § §

When the summer season ended Ted and Jackie finally took the chance to celebrate their marriage with a belated but fantastic honeymoon. Not surprisingly the destination was Canada, with the first stop being Montreal where Ted's bother Jack lived. By an amazing coincidence, on the flight out they met someone – in a country of nearly four million square miles! – who knew him.

A Scots Canadian who had been appearing on the This Is Your Life programme dedicated to his wartime commanding officer, boarded the plane at Prestwick. As they got chatting the Hockridges mentioned that they were going to see Ted's brother Jack and as they answered the Canadian's questions it became clear that they lived in the same area… then that they lived in the same road… and then that he and Jack were next-door neighbours!

Jack and his wife Margaret took Ted and Jackie to their holiday cabin in the Laurentian Mountains where they had an exhilarating time in the open air, canoeing, shooting rapids and drinking in the fabulous colours of autumn in maple tree country.

Then they took a suite on the train to Vancouver a three-day/four-night journey during which they were pampered with huge breakfasts of sausages, bacon, maple syrup and pancakes, as the awesome scenery of the Great Lakes, endless prairies and finally the Rockies passed by their window.

The homecoming was bitter sweet. Ted's brothers Brick and Murray, and their wives and families, meeting Jackie for the first time immediately loved her, and together they all enjoyed a warm, family atmosphere swapping tales and catching up with news. But sadly, after the death of Ted's father, his mother, whose memory had been badly affected by a stroke and who could not cope alone, was by now being cared for in a home.

Ted went to visit her. He says: "There was an amazing three or four minutes when her mind came out of its twilight world, recognising me and recalling the happy memories of days on the farm with her 'young Teddy'. And then she drifted away again with a smile on her sweet face. A few precious moments I will never forget." It became clear that Ted's father had been nursing his wife and trying to shield the family from the seriousness of her condition.

§ § §

When Ted returned to Britain he was cast as Abanazar, a 'baddie', albeit a sexy one, in his first provincial pantomime, Aladdin, at the Alexandra Theatre, Birmingham, and was asked back the following year to perform the role at Wolverhampton.

Christmas was coming and, as always with show people, there was a race to get off to enjoy a brief celebration; there is only 40 hours between the end of the performance on Christmas Eve to the matinee on Boxing Day. In that time, most have to pack up, drive home (sometimes hundreds of miles), prepare for Christmas Day and, having enjoyed that, grab a few hours sleep and make the mad dash to the theatre.

The Christmas of 1962, at Wolverhampton, was more frenetic than most for Ted and Jackie. They wrote cards and labels and wrapped presents in the dressing room between scenes. After Ted had got out of his costume, they joined the cast on stage to swap presents and have one glass of wine before the drive. Packed away in the car were champagne, and turkey and crackers. "As we set off," Ted recalls "it started to snow, and it was settling, but as I said to Jackie, Canadians are supposed to be able to cope with a bit of snow! We were heading for the newish M1, so we were thinking of being home in about two-and-a-half hours. But the snow turned to a full-scale blizzard and we were forced to reduce speed.

"Then it became difficult to keep the windscreen clear and, with the skidding, to keep the car in a straight line. Being Christmas Eve there were no lorries to squash down the snow and by 2.30 am we had not even reached the M1. The driving snow began to drift under the bonnet and shorted the electrics bringing us to a stop. So there we were enjoying our Christmas fare – cold sandwiches and a cup of warm coffee. This was long before mobile phones so we just sat there with no power and no heat.

"Suddenly, a police car on patrol emerged through the flurries of snow and two helpful bobbies got out and, shining their torches under the bonnet, dried everything off and got us going again. Their wives had both seen shows I had been in, so after autographs, and a few laughs, we gave them a bottle of vintage champagne to enjoy on their off-duty hours, and bade them grateful farewells."

The couple arrived home at 7.30 am and, after three or four hours' restless sleep, got up to arrange a high-speed Christmas, with Jackie's mother and brother helping. Up went the tree, up went the decorations, in went the turkey. Next day it was business as usual, after a pre-dawn departure to get back for that Boxing Day matinee. Ted insists: "There really IS no business like show business!"

CHAPTER FOURTEEN

Certainly, entertainers will agree that there is also no limit to the sorts of people that fame draws towards you, like moths to a lamp. Ted remembers one occasion when he and his MD Jack Martin fulfilled a cabaret booking at a big corporate occasion. After the performance they were invited to the directors' table and as the function ended, the boss of the company, a multi-million pound corporation, invited Ted and Jack back to his home for some food and a quiet drink. They accepted and when they reach the house, their host disappeared for about 15 minutes, leaving them chatting with his charming wife.

Suddenly he returned and burst into the room, flouncing around in an evening gown and wearing make-up. Ted says: "His wife didn't bat an eye! But we took one look at each other and made a very hasty exit."

Another time, while on a variety tour, Ted and the Taylor Maids, along with Bill Maynard, were invited to have a meal at the home of a well-to-do family, with other guests, who turned out to be dentists running a practice together. But as the evening wore on, and drinks flowed, hints were dropped about a huge bed in a room upstairs and there were suggestions that "the girls might like to see it."

Bill's worst fears were confirmed when he noticed that people had started disappearing upstairs two at a time. Ted recalls: "Bill said that although he was not a prude this was not his scene and I agreed – so we grabbed the girls and got the hell out!".

§ § §

*The catamaran we were sailing when we narrowly escaped the
disastrous storm when sailing on the South Coast.*

*Beau Geste and Sheba loved hurtling along with us at 35 miles an hour
in our Dowty speedboat. Jackie was three weeks away from giving birth
to Murray when this picture was taken.*

CHAPTER
15

"I explained to the officer that I was rushing because my wife was giving birth. He replied: "Follow me!"

Although Jackie was now 'retired' from show business she was enjoying supporting Ted who was busier than ever. They could now share every day together and plan their future home and family. They could also enjoy whatever leisure time they could grab. As Ted prepared for the 1963 summer season at Great Yarmouth, the unpredictable British weather and their love of boats combined to give them a nasty scare.

During his Torquay summer season the year before, Ted had done a Sunday concert at Weymouth Pavilion. After rehearsals, he and Jackie went for a walk along the harbour wall and came across an impressive catamaran. They struck up a conversation with the owner, Tom Lack, who turned out to be a fan and a builder of these boats at Mudeford, Christchurch. A lifetime friendship resulted from this chance meeting.

Tom, and Mary his wife, used to charter the 'cats' for sailing holidays and this greatly appealed to Ted and Jackie. Mary, who held a Masters Licence, coached them on how to sail the craft and before going off to Great Yarmouth for the season, they set off in one of the chartered cats, heading west, with the first planned overnight stop Poole Harbour. At 5 am the next morning they set sail for Weymouth. The sun was shining and the shipping forecast was favourable. Then came a shock. At 7 am they tuned in for another forecast and heard a Force 9 severe storm warning off Portland Bill.

Ted describes the next few hours…

"By this time we had sailed past Swanage and turned starboard to sail west to Weymouth after passing Durlston Head. We made a decision to head back to Poole immediately but for almost three hours everything was against us.

"The Spring tide was pouring out of the Channel at something like five knots and the wind was off our bow which didn't help. Even with our auxiliary engine we were only able to hold ourselves stationary while we wallowed in increasing swell. Finally, we began to creep forward, and north round Durlston Head. The seas and wind were rapidly building up as we pressed back into the comforting safety of Poole Harbour.

"Because we were on a catamaran with two hulls, we could 'park' it on the beach, and we chose the north side of Brownsea Island. Man, were we relieved to be there! Over the next 48 hours hundreds of boats along the south coast were wrecked by that storm. Thankfully, Jackie and I had plenty of supplies, and in particular some bottles of 'bubbly' so we didn't feel any pain! It was a great holiday."

When Ted joined Harry Worth and Billy Dainty for the summer season, he still had sailing on his mind and he and Jackie rented a house near the Broads – and bought a catamaran called Jumpahead (the speedboat was not allowed on the Broads).

It was now three years since Ted and Jackie had married, and Jackie had failed to conceive. She thought that the problem might lie with her and so she underwent a medical check-up. Everything was normal. Although Ted was already a father he decided that he should also be tested. He was shocked to discover that he was temporarily incapable of fathering a child.

He believed he knew why. He recalled an injury he had sustained in Blackpool when, in a mock wrestling match with Jack Douglas backstage, they crashed to the floor and Jack's knee had pounded Ted in 'the wrong place'. After some time, the pain had gone and Ted had forgotten about the incident until his problem was diagnosed. The treatment prescribed by the Harley Street specialist was simple but rather uncomfortable – and very comical! He was to apply ice packs to the appropriate area at regular intervals.

During the Yarmouth season, Jackie had a miscarriage, so they realised that Ted was now 'back on track'. She was referred to a specialist who had begun to make a name for himself in London. This was George Pinker who, much later, was to deliver Princes Harry and William. Jackie had to go into hospital for a small operation which cleared everything up and soon, to the delight of them both she was – in the words of one music paper making the revelation – 'infanticipating.' The good news was shared while they were in Bristol where Ted was co-starring in the Sleeping Beauty pantomime with his friends Morecambe and Wise, and Jackie joyously began to look forward to the fulfilment of a long-held dream, of motherhood.

After the pantomime finished, Ted was contracted to appear with Eric and Ernie on one of their TV shows. He was to play it straight (or try to!)

in a sketch as one of three Mounties on three dummy horses. But when one of his stirrups snapped, Ted was thrown headlong onto the floor – and could not get up as his other foot was trapped in the second stirrup. He tried to remember the director's instruction to play the straight man but how could he stay serious when Eric and Ernie were killing themselves with laughter as they looked down on him sprawling on the floor? What was worse is that the fall from grace could not be edited out; the show was live.

By the time Ted had started his summer season in Bournemouth, Jackie was heavily pregnant but it did not stop her enjoying high-speed rides on the Dowty speedboat, often to the Isle of Wight and back. Their dogs also enjoyed the trips, sitting on the bow of the boat with the wind in their faces as it scudded across the waves.

A couple of weeks before the baby was due, Jackie returned to London for an examination by Mr Pinker who suggested that she stay in the city as the baby might be arriving earlier than expected. Next day, she rang Ted in the morning to say: "I'm going in. But don't come up, you have shows to do – I'll be fine." Ted pretended to obey saying: "OK, I'll sit here and wait for news" before getting dressed and roaring up to London – well above the speed limit. A police motorcyclist stopped him near Basingstoke and when Ted explained that his wife was due to give birth, Ted was told "Follow me!" – and suddenly he had a high speed police escort as far as Heathrow (not being in the Met. he could go no further).

When Ted reached St. Mary's. Paddington, he was told that he had missed the big event by just 20 minutes. Jackie had given birth to a boy, David Murray.

Murray, as he is known, was born in September and Ian, who was now turning 21 and working for Pye Records, was delighted to have a half-brother. Jackie had now become friends with Eileen, something they had all worked at, and which made life so much easier for everyone, especially Ian.

It was to be a very hectic autumn for Jackie. As well as having to cope with a new-born baby, she organised a surprise 21st birthday party for Ian in October, inviting his mother and step-father as well as other members of the family, and friends. This was followed by Murray's christening in

November, and then preparations for moving out of the London flat to spend Christmas in a rented house outside Manchester during the pantomime season.

Ted was working away a great deal and he did not realise that Jackie had begun to suffer from post-natal depression. For about four months she was under par yet continuing to function as the mother of a young baby, and organiser, supporting Ted's busy schedule of shows and cabarets, and preparations for the next pantomime. She lost pounds in weight.

§ § §

Professionally, everything was going superbly. A plum date – and an honour Ted is proud of – was an invitation to sing for Sir Winston Churchill in a BBC TV tribute show, hosted by Noel Coward, to mark the statesman's 90th birthday. Ted sang one of Sir Winston's favourite songs. *Oh What a Beautiful Morning*. Later Ted was sent a copy of a letter from Sir Winston saying how much the show had meant to him.

The Manchester run of the pantomime Sleeping Beauty was hugely successful. It filled the Manchester Palace Theatre every night until April, Ted rented a house on the edge of the Peak District. The fresh air, country walks, and re-discovery of the places they had visited when courting, helped to lift Jackie's spirits.

Ted and Jackie had been talking of getting rid of their flat and buying a house. Morecambe and Wise were starring with Ted once more, and one day, when they were discussing houses Doreen Wise said: "Why don't you come and be our next door neighbours in Peterborough?" The idea had some appeal as the city was more or less in the middle of the country with improving motorway and good road connections and access to the main line of the railway system, but they did not think much more about it. Then Ernie and Doreen told Ted and Jackie that the house next door to them was up for sale and invited them up to stay for the weekend, so they could view it.

Ted was a little mystified when, at one point, the owner said discreetly to him: "I'm sorry but I can't accept the offer." Ernie had obviously been helping things along, negotiating the best price he could as a go-between. That night the Wises and the Hockridges went to a hotel for dinner and during the meal the neighbour they had met earlier walked through the door, stepped up to Ted and announced: "OK, I accept," to which Ernie replied: "Take it, Ted!". He did, and the Hockridges' long weekend in Peterborough is still being enjoyed four decades later.

That autumn, Ted appeared in London at the No. 1 cabaret venue of the time, the Talk Of The Town, in his first five-week season. This booking was the result of an earlier appearance when he stepped in for a week, at a moment's notice, for the American comedian Jackie Mason. The management's unanimous verdict was quoted at the time… "In five years only Frankie Vaughan has ever brought the house down as Edmund did. Even our waiters cheered!".

He was enjoying the big orchestra backing and appreciative audiences but the atmosphere was rather spoiled one night when two gentlemen, who, despite the lack of uniforms were obviously policemen, came into the dressing room and asked: "Have you any enemies, Mr Hockridge?". Ted said that there were none he was aware of. One of the policemen then said: "We've had a call from someone whose identity we do not know saying that they have a revolver and plan to shoot you".

Ted was assured that things would be all right but his accompanist, Jimmy Bailey, seemed less brave. "Did he mention me?" he asked nervously. Ted pictured Jimmy crouching on the floor in front of the piano with his hands working the keys above his head.

Jackie went into the audience with plain clothes policemen and anxiously watched every move; even someone moving a napkin set her nerves on edge. Ted found the whole thing a slightly eerie experience. He said there were more nervous chuckles in his act than usual – and he did find himself singing side on so that if the gunman appeared he would have less to shoot at. Eventually the man making the threats was caught and it emerged that he had been jailed in Canada by Mounties. Ted's brother Brick, who was in the Mounties, had been involved and when the man had visited England he had seen the name Hockridge and launched his plan for vengeance.

Jackie became pregnant again while Ted was doing a fourth summer season at Blackpool and returned to London. By the time he was installed in Sheffield, doing pantomime, with Roy Hudd, things started early again – and with a rush! She was taken to the London Clinic, and sedated before ringing Ted. In her drug-induced euphoric state Jackie wished him "Merry Christmas" – although it was March.

Concerned, Ted phoned during one of his breaks during the matinee and George Pinker, the obstetrician, sent him a message to say that Jackie was going into labour and to phone again in the interval, at 3.30pm. At 3.15 the baby had still not been born and Mr Pinker told Jackie: "Come on, Mrs H – your husband will be ringing in a few minutes!". When Ted phoned at 3.30, he received the news that the baby was a boy. Stephen James had been safely delivered.

After completing his evening performance, Ted hurried to his car and drove through the night to the London Clinic to greet the newcomer to the family and after a brief sleep, drove back to Sheffield – a very happy Dad – for the next matinee.

By the mid 1960s Ted had recorded scores of songs covering a wide range of music. including numbers from modern musicals and romantic ballads, folk songs, novelty songs, and spirituals.

On disc Ted had done *Largo al Factotum* in Italian, *Guantanamera* in Spanish and tuned in to the times by covering pop numbers that were enjoying big sales but brief popularity, songs like *Sixteen Tons* and *Stranger in Paradise*. And he had made his own impression on the charts with the singles *Hey There, Young And Foolish* and *No Other Love*.

Fans would also point to other 'unforgettables'… *I've Grown Accustomed To Her Face, Someday, Only A Rose, Some Enchanted Evening,* and of course, *My Boy Bill, the Soliloquy* from Carousel. They would also say that out of his 11 LPs and countless EPs and singles, the best of Ted's renditions are of songs by the greatest American song-writers, in which the emphasis is on distinctive melody married to superb lyrics, expressing feelings that might be romantic or even humorous but that immediately register with the hearer as something they have also felt. His power and clarity of diction gets the best out of what is there. Indeed there are fans who – half a century on – can remember the moment when they first heard Ted sing, and the effect his voice had on them.

Audrey Askew, a fan from Bedford, who confesses to being "the shyest person in the world", was first smitten by Ted's voice in 1941 when she heard him on the radio. In 1951 she first heard him sing If I Loved You and the impression he made was still fresh more than 50 years later. It was sung with such sincerity and intensity of feeling that it "tore at the heartstrings", she says. In the cause of celebrating a voice she believes to be unique, she overcame her natural reserve to appear on television showing her collection of "Edmundobilia"

By the late 1960s Ted had the chance to follow his records abroad to make personal appearances for fans in far-flung places. First stop – for Christmas 1966 – was Hong Kong and the fantastic Mandarin Hotel where he was to be the cabaret star for six weeks. Jackie had to stay at home with six-month-old Stephen, who was unwell at the time, and Murray, who was still a toddler. And there would soon be someone else to consider when plans were being made – a little boy called Cliff.

Clifford's mother and father were the caretakers of the Westbourne Terrace flats near Hyde Park where Jackie and Ted lived for some years after moving in 1956. Cliff was an endearing three-year-old when they first met him. They took to him immediately and felt great pity for him when, at six, his father died and Cliff arrived at the door of their flat saying: "My Dad went to heaven today."

Jackie and Terry would take Cliff to Kensington Gardens and Hyde Park where he would play with the dogs, Jackie's Beau Geste and Terry's Pidge and when Ted and Jackie had married they often took Cliff with them to give him a break at the seaside during summer seasons. After the Scarborough summer season of 1966, Cliff's mother also died. He was 12. Now, with two boys of their own, Ted and Jackie – against the advice of their London neighbours – were arranging to foster Cliff, whose older brother and sister had left home, and whose younger sister had been taken into care and then fostered. So Ernest Clifford Argyle joined the family; his achievements later in life were a source of great pride.

From the moment Ted set off for Hong Kong he was given VIP treatment. He was invited on to the flight deck of the Boeing by the captain, who had been in the Royal Canadian Air Force and, as an avid lover of aircraft, Ted savoured every moment of the 23 hours he spent there as the plane called in at Frankfurt, Rome, Bombay and Bangkok, before sliding down over the rooftops of Hong Kong and screeching to a stop at the end of the runway which can lead unwary pilots into the bay beyond.

Bruce Forsyth was just finishing his six-week stint at the world-famous Mandarin, so Ted had time to get over his jet lag. However, he called in on Bruce's last shows and weighed up the audience he would be facing, and then plunged into work, rehearsing with keyboard man Kenny Powell, and the resident Philippino band, which proved to be top class. His opening night struck the right chord. The sophisticated and well-travelled clientele appreciated the Cole Porter and Gershwin numbers, and the surprise of *Largo al Factotum*, thrown in for fun. After a month it was proving to be a very successful season and the newspapers took praise to lofty heights…

The Hong Kong Standard said: "Whatever songs Ted sings, he sings with magnificent effervescence, so superlatives are not out of order in describing him as perhaps the finest singer ever to grace a cabaret floor," and the China Mail chimed in with the view that this show was "one of the most wholesome and delightful cabarets presented at the Mandarin for many, many months."

Evidently Ted could do no wrong and one perk that resulted was a chauffeur-driven Rolls Royce which was made available to him for the duration of his stay. He put it to good use, exploring the area and even visiting the Gurkhas for a day on the Territories border, and enjoying a game of football with them.

But Ted was missing Jackie and the family, and maybe it was beginning to show. One of the directors of the Mandarin asked whether Ted might like some female company, alluding to the beautiful women who, evidently, were 'on the menu.' His reply probably came as a surprise. "Yes. I would like my wife to join me."

As Ted put it: "The enigmatic expression on his face never altered even though he was probably thinking: 'How very strange.' But then he politely asked: 'But why isn't she here?'.

"I explained that our youngest son Stephen had not been very well but I had heard from home that he was now OK. That was it. We went straight to his office where I phoned Jackie to tell her that our host was making arrangements for her to fly out – and within 36 hours the Rolls was whisking me to the airport."

Jackie was thrilled to be joining Ted although she was not looking forward to leaving her young boys but she quickly organised some help for her mother to look after them. Happy in the knowledge that they were in good hands she tosses a few things into a suitcase and was off.

The flight to Hong Kong, which then took the equivalent of a day and a night, and involved several stops, made Jackie a little apprehensive but eventually she began to relax. The lady who sat in one of the three seats grouped together got off at Frankfurt and as soon as she disembarked the young man next to Jackie made his move saying: "As we are going to spend the night together we might as well get acquainted…" Jackie was amused at first and thought that at least the man, who was with the Irish Consulate in Hong Kong, would make an interesting companion for a few hours of the flight. But things cooled when he suggested that they both get off at Bangkok, where he would show her some beautiful sights! She replied: "I don't think my husband would understand."

At the airport, Ted watched expectantly, trying to spot Jackie's long red hair among the incoming passengers. But there was no long red hair – and, it seemed, no Jackie. Then, suddenly, a girl dived into his arms. The long hair was now stylishly short but it was indeed Jackie, and thy left happily together for the remaining two weeks of pampering, fantastic food, horse racing, shopping for silks and dresses, and cultural outings.

By the time it was all over, they were pining for the children. They left the entertainment of the Mandarin's guests in the capable – if large, and sometimes bungling – hands of a friend, one Tommy Cooper.

§ § §

Arriving home from Hong Kong, Ted enjoyed a couple of weeks at home with the family before launching into another typically hectic year. During 1967 he would do months of touring in variety, and 20 Sunday concerts, countrywide. Added to these were a string of TV shows including Sunday Night At The Palladium, a Bruce Forsyth Special and a musical tribute event honouring Henry Mancini, in Cologne. In the same year, somehow Ted managed to squeeze in a five-week tour of South Africa and the role of Robin Hood in a repeat of the show that had been started at the Palladium. Somewhere along the way he managed to fit in a recuperative two-week family holiday in Majorca.

On the Forsyth TV show Ted was asked by the producer to join Bruce and Roy Castle in the finale, a complicated dance routine up and down a flight of stairs. Roy and Bruce, of course, were brilliant dancers. Ted was anything but; according to Jackie he most certainly had two left feet. But his nerves drove him on to rehearse the steps over and over again with the choreographer Pam Devis. He did not intend to make a fool of himself. After the show, the company was invited to watch a replay, and everyone fell about laughing when they saw that Ted was the only one of the three to get the routine completely right!

With him on the South Africa trip were two big stars of the day – Nina and Frederick, a Scandinavian singing duo. Nina turned out to be charming and easy to get on with but the whole company found that Frederick was hard work and offhand. However, they opened at Johannesburg City Hall, to a rapturous welcome and after a week flew to Durban, where they received an ecstatic response from the audience. Ted enjoyed the hospitality and fun, which included a get-together with a party of native dancers, a day in a safari park and a visit to a tribe where the chief had nine wives.

The show then moved to Cape Town for another week where Ted's

Leica camera was busier than ever on cable car trips up Table Mountain. Owing to the success of the show, Ted and company suddenly found themselves back in Johannesburg for another two weeks – and the management were now offering free holidays in Kruger National Park if the entertainers would stay on another month. All had other contracts to fulfil, so they had to decline. However, Ted's love of animals was indulged on a special trip before he flew home. "We were taken for one more wonderful day in a wildlife park where lions roared at us, and ostriches, protecting their chicks, tried to smash the windscreen of our host's stretched limousine. Great memories!'

Ted's trip to Cologne for the Tribute To Henry Mancini TV show was a fraught affair. He and Jackie flew on an increasingly foggy day in November. As they approached Cologne, the Comet made three unsuccessful approaches to the airport – the third almost turning into a disaster as they found themselves a few feet above the adjacent autobahn. Ted recalls: "Bursting through the fog, suddenly we could see cars just below us, under our wings. Thankfully the captain pulled away, and decided to land in Strasbourg."

The problem was that Strasbourg is about 200 miles south and Ted was due for rehearsal that afternoon; there were no trains available and although heavy snow was falling they found a taxi driver who was willing to drive them to Cologne. He turned out to be a veteran of Stalingrad, and had only one leg! "Thankfully", says Ted, "it was an automatic! Anyway, he got us there in time for rehearsals and for the filming. The show was a real joy to do, with songs like Mancini's *Moon River* to sing.

"Because of the fog there were no flights available to get us back, so we had a mad dash to Ostend for a ferry to take us across the Channel, before catching trains home so that we could re-pack, and set off for Bristol by car for the Robin Hood panto rehearsals, where I had a date with a sword – and a big one at that!"

As in all pantos, Robin Hood ended happily. But this production of a spectacular Palladium show could easily have ended in tragedy when the desire for drama and authenticity went dangerously awry. Billy Dainty,

Stan Stennet and Wyn Calvin provided comedy. Ted, cast as Robin, was the handsome, all-action hero. As such, he had some archery to perform in the show. This gave him no problem as he had handled bows as a boy in Canada but big, heavy swords were a different matter.

To achieve the excitement the producers wanted, Ted, and the Shakespearian actor playing the Sheriff of Nottingham, a man with experience in stage fighting, had to fight as if they meant it. They really wanted the sparks to fly. Ted and his 'enemy' were taught by experts in medieval swordsmanship, and the entire battle was choreographed. In around 20 progressive moves, one of them would bring down the sword, with a two-handed chopping movement, with the other parrying it by holding his sword horizontally. For it to work it had to be done with precision and as if there was real malice aforethought.

One night Ted sensed that the actor playing the Sheriff looked a little vacant and when they went into the fight, and Ted brought down a blow towards his head he was appalled to realise – in a split second – that the other man's sword was not in its defensive position. He managed to divert the sword as best he could towards himself avoiding smashing his opponent's head open. As it was, it just nicked the forehead and nose of the other fighter who, with children in the audience screaming, began to bleed before the curtain could be brought down.

Ted learned next day that, before he had gone on, the injured actor had been told some devastating news regarding his girl friend, and had been preoccupied with his personal life throughout the performance. He must have realised afterwards that he very nearly did lose his head over a woman.

When another run of cabaret appearances at the Talk Of The Town finished, Ted was to be involved in the making of history. He was booked to top the bill in cabaret for the first five cruises of the big, brand-new and beautiful QE2 which was to make four short proving cruises to establish staffing and service before making her historic maiden voyage to New York.

For the first voyage, the 'shake-down cruise' the Cunard staff and their teenage children were to be guinea pigs, and around 300 tradesmen were to sail, to finish interior work on the ship.

Ted enjoyed the family feeling on the cruise, to the Canaries, as everyone pitched in to ensure that once the ship's mechanical troubles were ironed out, the long-awaited New York voyage would be trouble free. Passengers were taken on for the other three short cruises and on one, Jackie was able to join Ted on board.

The guest list for the maiden voyage proper was dotted with VIPs from all walks of life, including ambassadors. Lord Mountbatten always sat at a front table when Ted was doing his cabaret act, and joined in lustily with the sing-songs and any other audience participation. The sound engineers on the ship were experimenting with early radio mikes and they were a constant pain in the ear for Ted. Part way through a song he would hear part of the conversation between two captains of ships passing nearby. Worse still, it would sometimes come out of the speakers and even battle with the sound from Geraldo's musicians!

The arrival of the QE2 in New York was a spectacular and noisy affair as naval boats, fire-ships, tugs, coastguard vessels, sight-seeing boats, and yachts formed an armada to escort her in. Police, Coastguard and Navy helicopters encircled her from above. Concorde had just had its maiden flight a week or so before the QE2 sailed. America was just about to see a third example of British brilliance. To the amazement of American fliers and spectators, an aircraft suddenly roared out of the sky, streaked across the funnels of the liner, rolled over, and suddenly came to a halt, hanging in mid-air, having decelerated from 600mph to nothing, apparently held up by an invisible force. America was seeing, in one glance, a fantastic new ship, and the very latest example of British aeronautical genius, the Harrier Jump Jet, dropping in dramatically from an aircraft carrier a couple of hundred miles away.

§ § §

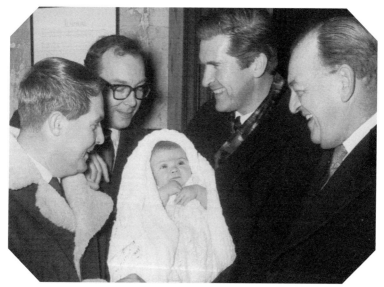

Murray's christening, with Eric and Ernie and J Ivor Griffiths the wonderful surgeon who saved my voice. He was Murray's godfather.

Clifford, the little boy we fostered, who made us very proud when he got an honours degree and went on to be a sports master.

"Have you heard the one about…?" Murray and Stephen show brotherly affection and a sense of humour at a birthday party.

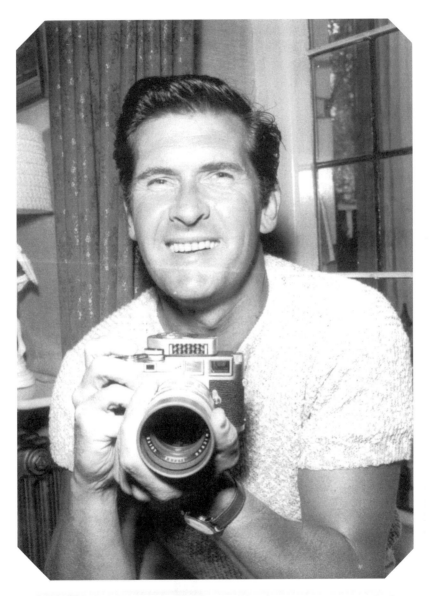

I had no interest in cameras after my wartime work in photography but when Murray came along I bought a Leica, the Rolls Royce of cameras, and set up a professional darkroom.

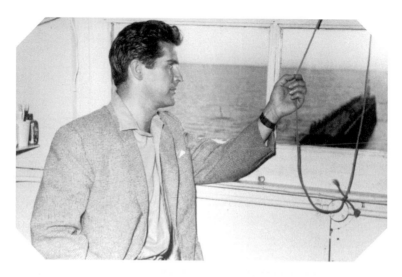

Jackie used the Leica to take this shot and has always loved it.

Making friends in South Africa, visiting tribes and safari parks.

Bruce Forsyth was just finishing his cabaret season when I arrived to do mine at the fabulous Mandarin Hotel in Hong Kong. The management flew Jackie out to join me (below) for what was a second honeymoon.

Right: While at the Mandarin I spent the day with the Gurkhas. I played soccer with them and even tried to master the bagpipes.

Left: The Palladium production of Robin Hood was later staged in Bristol and guess who played the lead.

CHAPTER 16

"I'm sorry. I don't see it that way. I have a wife and sons and I can't leave them behind."

In the summer of 1969 everything was coming up roses. Ted was in fine voice and enjoying another agreeable summer season, this time with Roy Hudd, in balmy Bournemouth. He had his family with him, and during their school holidays they enjoyed being part of the theatre life. Cliff – now 16 – was settled and secure and, fashionably equipped with a moped, got a temporary job delivering newspapers, while Murray and Stephen enjoyed the seaside, and being backstage.

Murray, who was only four, would go into the wings and listen to Roy Hudd's act, and he amazed the family, when he returned home, by borrowing Ted's reel-to-reel tape recorder and making his own recorded version of it, word for word, innuendos included.

In the autumn, Cliff had an accident that could have cost him his life. He was on his Lambretta on his way home from technical college when the car he had been following veered to the right and then left again, without signalling, and went into a driveway. Cliff was tossed over the vehicle and landed on his head but luckily landed on the only grassed section at the side of a busy road. He missed a lamp-post by inches.

Jackie prepared Cliff's favourite meal, steak and chips, but Cliff did not arrive. Then came a call from the hospital. Ted and Jackie raced to Cliff's side and found that though he was bruised and battered, and had broken his jaw, there was no brain damage; the open-face helmet he had been wearing had save his head – but not his face – from injury. His jaw was wired up and so steak and chips was off the menu. Instead Jackie had to liquidise his food until his jaw healed.

Out of the blue, Ted's career was about to undergo a dramatic change. He was called in to see Bernard Delfont at his office. There a plan was revealed. "Ted, I'd like to send you to Las Vegas" he said. Ted could see the reasoning behind the idea, and everyone knew that there was big money to be made out there, a point being proved by Tom Jones. But the suggestion came as a shock because moving to America was the last thing that Ted, as a devoted family man, wanted.

He expressed his reservations and Delfont was displeased. There was a strong hint that Ted should think hard about his decision but he needed no more time to think. "Sorry" said Ted "I don't see it the way you do. I have a wife I love, two little boys and an adopted son. I can't leave them behind and I wouldn't want them coming with me."

Delfont was adamant. "If you turn this down our contract is finished", he announced. Ted did, and suddenly was no longer under protective wing of the most powerful show business figure in the country.

Looking back, Jackie believes she can see how this break turned out to be so devastating, and how Ted's sense of loyalty had worked against him.

Ted's agent, Lillian Aza, a much-respected figure, with Stanley Holloway and Gracie Fields on the books, was very close to the Grades; in fact she ran their business when they joined up during the war.

Her connection with Lou and Leslie Grade and Bernard Delfont was beneficial for entertainers such as Ted when things were going right but her connections outside that empire were not very strong. So once Ted had burned his boats with Delfont, Lillian's ability to find him high-profile bookings was limited, Jackie believes.

Jackie says: "Ted is a typical Leo, and one quality they have is loyalty. He should have changed agents but he didn't want to and I believe that as a result he missed many opportunities."

The next couple of years were tough; in the Hockridge family archives they languish under the title "Doldrums". But Ted, who was trim (from isometric exercise), healthy (from careful diet and daily vitamins) and who was singing as well as he had done at any time in his career, did not intend to allow a 30-year career to peter out.

For two years, he sang in clubs, mainly, and then joined Dickie Henderson, Lionel Blair, and Peter Goodwright in a summer season at Eastbourne. He also became ultra mobile by buying a Winnebago, an American motor home, so that there was now no need to rent houses for the season, when they were having to live away from their Peterborough base.

The boys loved the idea that the mobile home could be parked right in the heart of the countryside as it was when they found a rural spot near Hailsham. Dickie Henderson, who was a golf addict, and his wife Gwyneth, made being away for the summer even more exciting by giving them their first golf lessons.

Soon afterwards, Cliff delighted the family when as a result of his hard work in compiling a thesis on the development of Peterborough, he was rewarded with a place at Loughborough College, which gave him training as a sports teacher. Although he was not very tall for a basketball player, he excelled at the game and became captain of the Northamptonshire Under 21s team.

The other two boys were also sports mad, both playing cricket and football. Stephen also played rugby and both are keen on fishing. Ted is also very keen on sport, and Jackie – whose policy has been "if you can't fight 'em, join 'em," has always had a great interest in sports of all kinds. She believes that it stemmed from her father's influence as he was an excellent athlete, a first class gymnast and swordsman, competing in the epée event at the 1920 Olympic Games in Antwerp. Murray and Stephen were also showing a talent for music and it seemed only a matter of time before they joined 'the family business.'

When, during the summer season, someone suggested that Ted should create a one-man show, Jack Martin the musical director got to work on some music with Ted, who chose a string of anecdotes to complete an entertaining package. One of the first performances was 'at home' – in the Key Theatre, Peterborough, and during the show, to warm applause, eight-year-old Murray was invited up to play the bongos.

The next summer season, at Southend, with Billy Dainty, was memorable because the golf and the fishing were good – in fact one day Jackie had her picture in the local paper after she caught a huge stingray!

Later in the year, Ted was to discover what it was like to work in the massive northern entertainment clubs that had evolved from the workingmen's clubs of Yorkshire. The clubs at Wakefield and Batley represented a new phenomenon. They were vast – and slightly posher – versions of prosperous smaller clubs, run in industrial areas by committees, and staging weekend shows (often after bingo!) starring some of the biggest names in entertainment.

Ted was to appear in these clubs over a period of three years and he noticed how the dress code of the audience changed over time. When he first sang, many men would be sporting dinner jackets and the women would be wearing evening dresses. When he next visited the men were in lounge suits and the women more casual and when he went back again, jeans and tee shirts dominated.

Ted was now recording for Decca, cutting several LPs including selections from the musical Camelot as well as Western Heritage, which was based on American songs telling how the West was won.

As they planned their 1975 summer season at Great Yarmouth, the Hockridges ordered a new 'home' – a 24-foot motor home called a Superior, manufactured by the firm that builds Greyhound buses. They parked this not far from Gorleston Golf Club, and here Dickie Henderson, who was also in the show, was able to continue to coach the boys. One evening when the boys had gone to practise, Jackie became concerned that they were not back and found them in the clubhouse with the regulars enjoying a yarn and a lemonade.

Murray and Stephen had a wonderful treat in the following year when Ted was invited to do cabaret on a Canberra cruise to the Greek islands. A plea was made to their school and it was agreed that they could have two weeks off so long as they wrote essays about their experiences.

Ted was regularly booked for cabaret over the next few years and Jackie joined him whenever she could. They loved history, people and places and relished the chances Ted's career gave them to see the world. Cairo and the Pyramids, Elba, Naples, Pompeii, and Vesuvius – where Jackie had her newest and best hat blown off when she rode in a cable car! – all proved to be wonderful experiences. He says that he often felt especially privileged to be having such a wonderful time "all because some people seem to think that I make a pleasing noise."

§ § §

In the late 1970s both Murray and Stephen were progressing well with their music and it seemed clear that they would follow their parents into 'the business'. During concerts and cabarets Murray, who was quickly developing as a drummer, was encouraged by Dad and MD Jack Martin to join them as part of their backing group on stage. Meanwhile Stephen, who wanted to get in on the act, had learned to play the bass guitar and Jack had patiently helped him to learn the bass parts for Dad's act.

Ted was asked to do some promotional concerts for Hammond, the organ company, when Bryan Rodwell was their chief demonstrator. They had also arranged for Ted to record an LP for them, with Jack on the piano and Bryan on the organ, backed by a bassist and drummer.

The day before the recording was Stephen's ninth birthday and Jackie had arranged a party for him and his friends at the house. It was March, and too cold to go outside, so they had games in the large playroom at the house. The children were enjoying relay races with dad and mum at either end of the lines, overseeing their safety, as there were French windows. They were asked to stop while ice cream was brought. But, being kids, they didn't!

Suddenly there were screams from the room. Murray had slipped and skidded through one of the panes of glass, and his left arm had been damaged as he pulled it back. Dad organised an improvised tourniquet, using a clean tea cloth to hold together the damaged skin and muscle and Murray was whipped off to hospital.

On arrival they were asked whether he had eaten lately, but before Mum and Dad could answer, Murray replied, "I've only had six sausages and three lemonades." As far as he was concerned that was nothing, but it was too much to allow him to be operated on right away. During the night he had forty-eight stitches inserted; luckily no tendons had been severed and the injury did not jeopardise his future as a percussionist.

Ted and Jackie stayed with him until he came out of the anaesthetic and was comfortable. They then snatched a few hours sleep before Ted set off for London and the recording studio, where he did his weary best.

He made great progress and in 1980, after Ted had finished a season singing in Blackpool, Stephen made his stage debut at Lewisham with Dad, Jack, and Murray and played immaculately, giving an apparently nerveless performance (despite the internal tremors he later confessed to having!). Jack was thrilled with him and was really enjoying having the boys as part of the team, and the audience adored the idea of lads of 14 and 16 being in the show.

Over the next two summers, in shows at Eastbourne and Scarborough, Murray and Stephen – who as youngsters had to have a licence to do limited stage work – accompanied Dad, with Jack at the piano. They also enjoyed football matches with the stage staff and parties with the dancers; they were growing up fast. While at Eastbourne, the Congress Theatre staged an extra show in honour of Princess Margaret, and after their appearance with their father and Jack Martin, the boys were presented to the Princess.

During the Scarborough season, Ian and his girlfriend joined the family for a couple of weeks. It was a happy, family-centred time. Mum and Dad organised fishing trips for them all, catching cod that lurked around wrecks ten miles out in the North Sea (on one outing, Murray caught a twenty-pound ling cod). Over the weeks, Jackie struck up a friendship with Laurel Brighty, a dancer, who was to be instrumental in laying the foundation for Jackie's new 'career'.

Laurel was a keen keep-fit enthusiast, having to keep in shape for dancing. Jackie, as a former dancer, was nearing 50 and was at the stage where she felt she had to fight back against the ageing process. "Things were beginning to go southwards, and it was time to do something about it!" said Jackie. They had the idea of starting a fitness class but geography was a problem – Laurel had a panto to do, and anyway, she was based in Kent while Jackie, of course, lived in Peterborough. The pantomime finished, Laurel came to Peterborough and she and Jackie held classes four times a week. Although Jackie now says that the classes were the best thing that ever happened to her, laying the foundations of fitness for years to come, she had to go through the pain barrier. "I thought my muscles would never recover!" she says.

They doubled the number of weekly classes and Jackie continued to teach. After 18 months, Laurel married and moved away, but Jackie continued on her own devising and leading weekly sessions for twelve years, which kept her trim and gave her the appearance of a woman 20 years younger than her true age.

As Jackie's keep-fit 'career' took off, Ted was about to star in a musical, more than 25 years after his last, Pajama Game at the Coliseum. The show was South Pacific, and he fulfilled a lifetime ambition when he was offered the lead part as Emil de Becque in a new production at the Connaught Theatre, Worthing.

The theatre was council-owned and their policy restricted any show to a maximum run of two months. But the production, which starred Hilary Tindall (of the TV series The Brothers) opposite Ted, proved such a crowd-puller that efforts were made to find a string of theatres for a tour. Most theatres were booked and so the idea faltered but the wonderful songs and the public approval really whetted Ted's appetite for more work in musicals, his first love.

When he was cast as the Emperor of China in a production of Aladdin, staged by the 'king' of pantomime Paul Elliott, at the Shaftesbury Theatre, London, Ted was delighted to find some of his favourite songs from Kismet incorporated into the production. So although he never appeared in the musical itself, he had the pleasure of doing such beautiful numbers as *And This Is My Beloved*.

One night was devoted to a special performance for charity and the Duke of Edinburgh attended and met the cast on stage afterwards. Amazingly, Prince Philip recalled having heard Ted sing one of that night's songs at a Royal Command Performance about 20 years earlier.

Ted's memory of what was for him an enjoyable show to be in was marred some time later by the accidental death of Roy Kinnear who had been in the cast, with Richard O'Sullivan and Jill Gascoine and Lynsey de Paul.

After being reunited with the QE2, for another cruise, and with friends Frankie Vaughan and Bernard Braden, a fellow Canadian, who were doing cabaret on the ship, Ted had the offer of another lead part in a musical – again at the Connaught. It was in the Sound of Music, a show he had been approached for when he had ended a seven-year spell doing musicals in the West End, back in the Fifties, Then, instead, he had been signed up for the Palladium by Bernard Delfont . Now, for two months, he was Count von Trapp, starring with Isla St Clair.

Again the show was a great success and once more there was talk of trying to take it one tour. However, Ted was under contract for the Aladdin pantomime in Manchester, this time with an assortment of 'names' – Su Pollard, Matthew Kelly, Ted Moult, Anneka Rice, Derek Griffiths and Tommy Trinder.

Pantomime can produce some interesting combinations on stage and, to their amusement, when Ted and Su Pollard were brought together they found that presenting a united front in terms of sound was not easy. Because Su had a small (but sweet) voice, her microphone volume had to be set high; Ted's was turned down low because he needed very little help with volume. The problem was that when they came near each other, Su's microphone would suddenly pick up Ted's voice, resulting in a startling change of volume for the audience!

When the round of cabaret appearances, concerts and one-man shows resumed, Ted discovered that Jack was becoming unwell, and there was an alarming incident when they took the one-man show to Southport. In the car park before the show, Jack fell down. Although he seemed all right when he was stationary, when he tried to walk he lost his balance. A doctor was called in and diagnosed an inner ear problem and gave him some pills. Despite feeling so unsteady, Jack was determined that the sell-out show would go ahead.

He insisted his piano playing was not affected and went out and proved it by providing faultless accompaniment for two hours. But in order to avoid the loss of balance, he had to be installed at the piano while the curtains were closed, and helped off the stage when the curtains came down at the end of the show. Sadly, Jack became increasingly unwell and after 17 years of happy co-performing, to Ted's bitter disappointment, he was forced to retire.

§ § §

When Harry Secombe's popular travelling TV show Highway visited Peterborough, it was obvious that one of the singers would be Ted who was now a 'local' but what happened was to sow the seed of an idea that was to change the lives of Ted and Jackie. The producer also asked Murray and Stephen to appear on the show and to do one of their original songs, along with two local boys who were in a band they had at that time.

When it was realised that Jackie had appeared in musicals, the idea of having Jackie singing with Ted came up. Jackie, who had been out of show business for 25 years, was less keen. Not surprisingly after all that time she was worried about picking up the threads, and, anyway, she was generally sceptical about wives working with husbands who were established stars. But she was persuaded and so they all went down to Wembley to record the numbers.

Jackie and Ted sang a duet – *If I Loved You* – and Jackie sang *When I Marry Mr Snow*, both songs from Carousel, the show they had been in when they first fell in love 34 years before. Murray and Stephen sang their composition *Beautiful Girl*.

The question asked after the TV appearance was: "Why aren't the family doing a show together?" Among those asking it was Harry Secombe, was an old friend. They had first met many years before when Ted asked Harry to be a guest on his BBC show I Hear Music, when they sang the famous baritone-tenor duet from La Boheme.

This might just be something for the future. Meanwhile Ted had singing dates abroad. After appearing in a TV show in Amsterdam, on the same bill as the jazz trombonist Don Lusher, Ted – taking Jackie with him – enjoyed a five-day working holiday to Copenhagen, where he sang in the Tivoli Gardens with the Danish Symphony Orchestra. Returning to Holland, Ted joined June Bronhill and two German opera singers, who although outstandingly good, received a muted welcome from the audience. Ted, by contrast, was given rousing cheers. He was later told by management that the audience were showing the residue of ill-will from the days of the war when the Canadian army played their part in kicking the Nazis out of Holland.

CHAPTER SIXTEEN

Yet another musical role – Ted's seventh – was waiting in the wings. While appearing in pantomime at Wimbledon he had a meeting with the director of the Chichester Theatre who was planning a revival of Annie Get Your Gun, and in need of a Buffalo Bill. Ted was pleased to oblige, especially as Chichester had such a high reputation for first class theatre. "And after all, at 69 I was ripe and ready!" he says.

A minor complication was that Ted was already committed to starring in Aberdeen in variety. Having missed a week of rehearsals while he was in Scotland, he came off stage after the last performance at 10 30 pm and, with Jackie, drove through the night to Peterborough. Murray then took the wheel and got his Dad to the rehearsal room at Chichester by mid-morning the next day… a total of 520 miles of driving – and no sleep.

An invitation had gone out to Irving Berlin to attend the opening night of Annie Get Your Gun but he settled for a message of goodwill and a visit from some of his associates. The eminent songwriter was, after all, 99! After the opening a glowing report was sent on to Berlin.

The plan for the show was that after a few weeks at Chichester it would do a tour of the provinces and arrive in London in early winter to be an alternative attraction to pantomime, as it was a show that could be enjoyed by the entire family. But pressure from New York to skip the touring and move straight into London overcame resistance here and the Aldwych was booked to take the show.

The cast moved to Plymouth for re-staging and shaping, to fit the show into the Aldwych which is more of a playhouse than a venue for a big musical (just one of the 'props' was a railway carriage which nearly filled the stage)

The move to London, in summer, seemed to be vindicated by booming early ticket sales and there were hopes that the show would run for a year or more. But in mid-autumn the crisis between America and Libya was intimidating US citizens, who were afraid to travel. Gadaffi announced in September that he had sent arms to Nicaragua to help them to fight America, and Arab terrorists shook Paris with a series of bombs, forcing the country to impose new rules for foreign visitors.

Americans had been buying around a third of all tickets for the show which played to packed houses during the summer and autumn. A long run was looking very promising. But suddenly the American tourists were no longer arriving. Before the highly profitable panto season had begun, the revenues had turned into deficit and the show was forced to close. As a result of this the entire cast missed out that year on Christmas season bookings.

Concerts and cabaret filled most of the new year until Ted was booked to take again the role of the Emperor in Paul Elliott 's production of Aladdin. And so he found himself once again back in Plymouth, this time working with Bernard Cribbens, Andrew Sachs and Anita Harris.

While down there, Jackie was reunited with a little bit of her ancestry.

Jackie's father Kenneth Jefferson was an American, born in Boston, Massachusetts. But the family considered themselves more Canadian than American and came to Britain, when he was 12. They settled in Oxford, the children were educated there and the whole family became 'English'.

Jackie was aware of links with the name Brewster and the Pilgrim Fathers, and recalls that as a girl, a legacy used to come to her family every three months from a distant aunt, Caroline Brewster, also of Boston. Kenneth, who was a captain in charge of PE for the British Army, had a sister. Jackie remembers that her aunt believed herself to be one of the 'Grand Dames of America', an honour only bestowed on descendents of those who sailed on the Mayflower, which in 1620 landed at Plymouth, Mass., having travelled from Plymouth, Devon. While in Plymouth, Ted and Jackie were having dinner with Angela Rippon and her husband when the subject of Jackie's ancestry came up. After the meal, Angela took them down to the harbour – and showed Jackie the commemorative plaque on which the Mayflower passengers are listed. There was William Brewster's name.

§ § §

CHAPTER
17

Paul the MD lived with the family working on music involving every member of the family

Returning home to Peterborough, Ted and Jackie gave some thought to Harry Secombe's suggestion about Jackie joining Ted on stage. Although Jackie was super fit for a woman of her age (thanks to those exercise classes!) and had kept her beauty, she was hesitant about stepping back into the profession she had left 28 years before to start a family. When Ted brought Jackie on stage to do a 'guest' spot, the welcome she received from the audience, and the applause after her singing, lifted her spirits and reassured them both that they were on target, and that Harry's suggestion had been an excellent one.

One enormous strain on Jackie was that her mother Gwen, by then a widow, was seriously ill. When Ted and Jackie had moved to Peterborough, Gwen, who was separated from Jackie's father, had been invited to join them. They had found her a flat about a mile away from their house. Gwen loved the boys and had been only too happy to babysit through the years, leaving Jackie assured that they were in safe hands whenever she went away with Ted, often to help with the driving. Although Gwen, during her illness, enjoyed seeing the family show evolve in rehearsals, sadly she died before they made their debut.

Ted and Jackie had two strong allies in the new venture in what was to be The Hockridge Family Show. One was Peter Foot, who was then Ted's agent and who believed passionately in the potential of the new show and secured 20 dates at the Hippodrome, Eastbourne, for summer of 1988.

The second was Paul Burnett, who had been one of Bernard Delfont's musical directors, and an old friend of the family. Paul agreed to help shape two entirely different shows, working out orchestrations and building in solo spots, and duets, for Ted, Jackie, Murray and Stephen.

This was a massive job, involving 60 songs, and the only way to tackle it was for Paul to live with the family so that they could work intensively every day. Paul was on piano and a young keyboard player, Sep Cipriano – one of the local boys who had appeared with Murray and Stephen with their band on the Highway programme – was drafted in to augment Murray on drums and Stephen on bass guitar.

Ted, approaching 70, was having the time of his life and Jackie was enjoying singing such great hits as Bewitched, Bothered and Bewildered. She even choreographed a dance routine to do with Ted! The Hockridge Appreciation Society warmly welcomed the family format, as entertainment that not only enabled them to see their hero but also his wife and children – in a happy and wholesome show that could be enjoyed by entire families. Ted and Jackie injected glamour and romance, and the boys – Murray, Stephen and Sep – added appeal of a different sort, and musicianship of the highest order.

Murray's rendering of New York, New York while drumming always drew big applause and Stephen's touching solo *Someone To Watch Over Me* brought out the maternal instincts of older women in the audience! The boys also caused an enthusiastic ripple with the High Society duet *What a Swell Party This Is.*

There was nostalgia too. When Ted sang his hit, Hey There, instead of the having a tape recording of Ted's voice providing responses, Murray provided this side of the musical conversation for his father. Ted's voice was as strong as ever, and he took delight in surprising the audience with full volume renditions of *Largo al Factotum*, taken at full speed, and by occasionally dispensing with the microphone to show that there was lots of life in the old dog yet! Without setting out to make a point, Ted and Jackie were proving that the worst thing that people reaching retirement age can do is to fall into the stereotype of being prematurely "old".

On stage, the couple gave full rein to the affection they felt for each other, and the pride they had in their offspring and the audience responded approvingly.

They glowed even more warmly when the couple's Labradors – first Cindy and her eventual replacement Stella – made appearances on stage.

The run-up to Christmas of 1988 was already clouded by the death of Jackie's mother. Then, two days before Christmas, Cindy died. She had made dozens of appearances in shows and was a true member of the family and so the house felt empty during that festive season. Stella joined the family – and, eventually, the professional line-up – in the Spring. Both dogs played their part in supporting Ted's favourite charity, Guide Dogs for the

Blind, for which the Hockridge 'team' have raised thousands of pounds.

Among Ted's stories about their beloved – and star-struck! – pets was one about Cindy, and an incident when he appeared in The Sound Of Music. Cindy travelled everywhere with them, and like Stella, who was to follow in her paw prints, grew to recognise the finale music, and would be eager for attention.

One night, Ted forgot to shut Cindy in his dressing room, and when – after taking bows and curtain calls – the cast launched into a reprise of *Climb Every Mountain* suddenly the skirts of the singing nuns seemed to bulge out in turn before, to whoops of delight from the audience, Cindy finally appeared from under the skirt of a rather surprised Mother Superior.

Ted was appearing in what was to be his last pantomime that Christmas and he gained some comfort from the fun he had with one of his co-stars, Jeffrey Holland. They became friends and discovered that among the many things they had in common was a liking for cribbage. This became so competitive that they nearly missed entries because they were so deeply absorbed!

§ § §

It was in the following summer, as editor-in-chief of the Peterborough-based national magazine YOURS (and a music-lover) that it struck me that just down the road from our offices lived someone who would make a great interview – Ted Hockridge. The readers, most of whom are retired, enjoy reading about those who remain active in later life, and catching up with the lives of stars who were prominent when they were younger.

As we talked, an immediate bond was established. Views seemed to coincide, interests were explored and trust was affirmed. Ted and the family appeared on the cover of the magazine and after seeing the family show, from somewhere came an idea that the family and the magazine could work together.

Together we worked out a sponsorship arrangement with YOURS telling readers where the shows were, Peter Foot – Ted's agent at the time – booking the theatres and Ted, who was by then a reader, telling the audience, briefly, that there was a magazine out there that helped people to be positive after retirement. The magazine's message was that it was for the 'young at heart', and Ted would sing a few bars of the song of that name before mentioning the magazine

When the family show went on the road, they carried what they needed for the concert. Ted had a tick list to check that every item was on board before heading for the venue for their performance. He has remarked that this was a time when the Hockridges were a family of wheels and when you consider that in one four-month spell of family shows they covered 6,000 miles, the description seems appropriate.

The family would set up all their gear and do sound checks, present two hours of entertainment and then make the long journey home, often a long-distance drive. Whatever the time, they would usually head straight back to Peterborough along empty roads arriving home at three or four in the morning.

As the shows were so far from home, to forget something was a major problem. One night, in Skegness, as the family settled into the theatre, Stephen – who was dressed in casual clothes – suddenly realised that he had left his stage clothing at home. He checked the time – almost 5 30pm. The race was on to get to a clothes shop before it shut.

He managed it, hurriedly buying gear he would never have normally chosen in a million years presentable enough for the show but hardly his style! But as the saying goes, it was "all right on the night."

On another occasion, Murray and Stephen – both keen sports fans – realised that they would be on stage while England were playing Cameroon in the quarter final of Italia '90. Murray had the prefect solution. He placed a small TV set behind the bass drum, out of sight of the audience and during the show kept up with the action! The family finally owned up to the audience at the end of the show, telling them – to cheers – that England had won.

In August of 1989, with the Family Show well and truly established Ted managed to ease up for a moment to celebrate his 70th birthday, with the help of members of his Appreciation Society, who prepared a book of mementos and information recording his career, and tributes from the world of show business.

Among those sending congratulations were Syd Lawrence, Robert Farnon, Ron Goodwin, Ernie Wise, fellow Canadian Jackie Rae, David Jacobs, and Jane Martin, Ted's leading lady in Carousel who signed herself "July Jordan" and reassured Ted that, at 70, he was "still a gorgeous leading man."

There was also one long and glowing tribute from someone in the world of art – Ted's friend, Terence Cuneo, or Terry as he preferred to be called. Since they had first met in 1953, he had become a hugely collectable artist, and painter of Royals. He had painted the Queen at least a dozen times and had always included a tiny mouse tucked away somewhere in the detail. Having completed one more royal painting he was once asked by the Queen: "And where is the mouse this time, Mr Cuneo?".

His letter recounted the fun they had enjoyed together – the day when Ted became the artist's assistant, climbing up scaffolding in the Science Museum to help Terence 'slap colour on' to a whopping, sixteen-foot canvas, and of the time Terence – a renowned painter of locomotives – drove an old French steam loco in Peterborough and couldn't stop pulling the whistle cord.

The artist had just celebrated a birthday landmark himself. He turned 80 before Ted reached 70 and his special day had been marked by the display of more than 1,000 of his canvasses in galleries in Pall Mall, London.

Jackie planned a secret birthday party as a surprise for Ted, inviting the last remaining brother, Murray Snr, who was now getting a little fragile, along with Luanne, to look after him (Grace, his wife, was not well enough to travel from Vancouver). Jackie told Ted that she had invited Terry up for a small dinner party. And she got him out of the house for a few hours by suggesting he took Terry to Burghley, the historic house near Stamford, just 12 miles away. Terry was asked to steer Ted back home by 2 30pm for the surprise celebration.

All appeared to be going well with the four boys, Ian, Cliff, Murray and Stephen, arriving with their girl-friends, along with Murray and

Luanne. Other guests arrived but 2 30 came, and went. An hour later, the guests were drowning their sorrows.

Finally – an hour late – the birthday boy arrived to enjoy his surprise. Terry explained that he had great trouble restraining Ted who wanted to extend the trip by showing him another local beauty spot. In the end, he had feigned exhaustion, and Ted had relented and headed for home.

Terry's birthday book tribute took Ted and Jackie back to the mid-fifties when Terry, who by that time had become a friend, said, with a mischievous twinkle, that he'd like to propose to Jackie. Ted looked at him quizzically until Cuneo said: "Yes, I'd like to propose to Jackie…that she should be my model for my portrait for this year's Royal Portrait Society exhibition!"

Jackie accepted and 'The Lady With the Green Gloves' was the outcome, a portrait that toured the world, being shown in galleries in Los Angeles, New York and Buenos Aires. Twenty years later Terry held a champagne party at his home in Hampton Court for close friends and fellow artists and after a convivial evening he asked for silence, and for the company of around 40 to move to his studio, where, he said, he wanted them to witness an act intended to show his deep affection for one of their number.

They entered what looked like a small museum. There were paintings, statuettes, ancient guns hung on the walls, and mementos of world travels, along with easels, oils and brushes.

He announced that 20 years before he had painted a special picture of a special person, and he had treasured it since. Then, with a dramatic swoop, he whisked off a sheet and revealed 'The Lady With The Green Gloves', saying: "It's yours, Jackie – provided I can always borrow it back for any future shows."

§ § §

In the early Sixties I bought this Bentley second-hand. It ate up petrol and was heavy handling so I got rid of it, not knowing then that it had been the Duke of Edinburghs's car when he was in the navy in Malta.

By the late Sixties, Ian, my son from my first marriage, was doing well in record promotion. While working for CBS he introduced us to Andy Williams

A family of golfers – having been introduced to the game by Dickie Henderson and his wife. Below: Having fun with Dickie and Gwyneth who became great friends during summer seasons at Eastbourne and Yarmouth

*Jackie ran dance exercise classes for twelve years.
How about this for 55 years of age? Gorgeous!*

As Emil De Becque, in a clinch with Hilary Tindall in South Pacific.

Enjoying a chat with Captain Bill Warwick when I topped the cabaret bill on the maiden voyage of the QE2, sailing from Southampton to New York. 25 years later I did a QE2 encore!

Below: Fans join me as we approach New York harbour on the maiden voyage.

CHAPTER 18

*Cruising to calmer waters –
and a QE2 reunion*

The first three years of the 1990s saw the Family Show flourish. Audiences throughout Britain seemed to be struck by two facts when they saw the show. First, that the passing of the years did not seem to have greatly affected Ted's voice, and, secondly, that Ted, Jackie, Stephen and Murray were not only in harmony on stage; they were a genuinely close and happy family. Ted and Jackie have always said: "They are not just wonderful sons but also our best pals."

As well as singing and playing in the family shows, Murray and Stephen were developing their own music. They converted part of the family home into a sound--proof studio and song-writing suite, equipping it with the latest computer-aided recording technology. They created a variety of music under various pseudonyms, both in recordings and live performances.

One blow to the family had been the death of a very talented musical associate called Bryan Rodwell, a keyboard player par excellence, and a renowned jazz musician and orchestrator. He was also in great demand as a demonstrator for organ manufacturers and for many years led a touring jazz band.

When Paul Burnett had been unable to play as accompanist, Bryan used to step into the breach. By a strange coincidence Paul and Bryan came from the same Yorkshire town, Keighley, and attended the same school, although at different times, because of their ages. Bryan's brilliant flair for music meant that he could absorb a score on sight, and although he was a dazzling soloist, his playing for singers was empathetic and embellishing, rather than attention-grabbing. Ted had known him from the Fifties and his loss was keenly felt, especially as the family had greatly valued his sense of humour and companionship.

And now Paul Burnett, who was in his seventies, and who had given such wonderful support in every way, was himself not 100 per cent fit and had to retire.

As well as doing the family show, Ted, now in his early seventies, and Jackie were also being booked for cabaret spots. When Ted was 73 they were contracted for a week's cabaret at the Forte Grande Hotel in Dubai and for the trip they 'borrowed' Barry Cryer's MD, Colin Sell. It turned out to be quite an adventure.

Ted says: "I still have a Canadian passport and visited Canada house in London to check on any visa requirement. "No visa necessary", I was told. But how wrong they were!

"When we arrived, at midnight, Jackie with her British passport went straight through but the immigration people took me to one side and pondered over mine. Suddenly, a military gentleman took me by the elbow and led me into the reception hall, saying that I could not go through without a visa. I was then parked on a wooden bench for the night, with two armed sentries watching over me. I was virtually under arrest. I tried a touch of John McEnroe-type vehemence ("You CANNOT be serious!") but that did not seem to go down too well.

"Jackie was allowed to join me, and she quietened me down – but, man, was I mad! Most of my fury was directed at the girl in Canada House who had given me wrong information.

"Jackie went into a hotel where she alerted the man who had organised the contract and he in turn told the hotel but they were powerless to do anything until the morning when they would contact the British Consulate. Meanwhile, until I was released, hotel sandwiches were brought to the airport and passed through the grill to 'the prisoner'. First thing next morning, there was immediate action and I left 'jail' just before noon.

"After 30 hours without sleep we were both exhausted and ready to take the next plane home but we soon recovered. We arrived home three days before our family Christmas."

While Ted and Jackie fulfilled bookings outside the family show, Murray and Stephen had also begun to play in a line-up that involved keyboard player Adrian Titman – and Adrian joined the family outfit for a series of concerts that took them all over Britain. They fitted in a 10-week season at Eastbourne at one end of the country, and put in appearances at Kirkcaldy and Kilmarnock over the border. With them always was Stella the Labrador who, when rehearsals were going on, would tour the auditorium sniffing each row of seats in turn, looking every inch a sniffer dog. "But" says Ted "we have had to admit that she was simply being a typical greedy lab, and looking for grub!"

Stella, a name that means "star", lived up to her moniker. When it came to her turn to go on stage she knew her music cue. Jackie says: "I would finish my duet with Ted, *They Can't Take That Away From Me*, and then go to the dressing room where she would be anticipating her appearance. Then she'd patiently wait in the wings until Ted finished *Seventy-Six Trombones*, and join him on stage where there was a little bit of business between them while she sat there looking cute. Everyone loved it. Then off she came to a waiting stage hand or stage manager who would follow her as she led them to the dressing room where she knew a little treat was waiting.

One day, out of the blue, came a call from Cunard. They said that as Ted had topped the bill on the first five cruises, they would like him to do the cabaret on a celebration 25th anniversary cruise to New York – and Jackie was invited to go too. They had committed to a booking which was overlapped by the trip but Cunard said they would fly the Hockridges back after five days of the voyage so that they could fulfil the date in Britain.

They had planned to enjoy food and wine and relaxation before the night on which they were to sing but it was not long before the sea began to boil and hundreds of people on board began to feel unwell – and Jackie was one of them ("As usual 'sailor' Ted was in his element !" she says, recalling that the cabin TV made things worse by showing the ship heaving up and down and rolling from side to side – "just like my stomach!"). Luckily there was enough time before their show for the weather to improve and Jackie to get her sea-legs, and they were able to enjoy a memorable concert – and the performances of fellow artistes George Shearing and the jazz singer Marion Montgomery.

When they arrived in New York a stretch limo was waiting to take them to the airport. They arrived at Heathrow at dawn, got in the car and raced up to Cheshire where the boys – their backing group that night – were setting up equipment ready to go into rehearsal.

CHAPTER EIGHTEEN

Cabaret over, they packed up to drive back to Peterborough, grabbed a few hours' sleep, then set off for Lowestoft where the Family Show was billed, before finally leaving for home, bringing a crazy 48-hours to a close.

When they were asked back again by Cunard, this time to do their 1001st cruise, to the fjords of Norway, once more it was their bad luck to have another prior date clashing. Cunard said that they would still like them to do the first leg, and so, after doing their cabaret on the first stage of the trip, they were once again flown home, this time from Oslo.

Murray and Stephen had left the Family Show by this time to concentrate on their own career, song-writing and developing a new band. After the Oslo cruise, Adrian secured a job playing in Dallas and Steve Hession became MD and arranger for Ted and Jackie in the remaining years before retirement.

In January,1996, they lost their dear friend Terry Cuneo who was almost 89 and who had been ill for some time. Terry's family asked Ted and Jackie to sing at the memorial service in London an event that turned out to be as amusing as it was touching. In fact, the congregation at the church of St Martin's-in-the-Field rocked with laughter at the hilarious memories that were recounted by various friends, senior Army officers, and by fellow artist David Shepherd. Ted and Jackie sang one of Terry's favourite songs, the Carousel anthem *You'll Never Walk Alone*. The 'audience' joined in and – most unusually for music in church – there was enthusiastic applause.

What followed gave Ted and Jackie comfort in their loss, and made them wonder whether the artist with the habit of hiding a mouse in his pictures was trying to tell them something.

"Terry believed in such things as life after death and he had promise: 'I'll try and come back and haunt you.'" Arriving home after the memorial event, Ted and Jackie pulled into their driveway and as the automatic light came on they saw, on the bird table near where the car stopped, a field mouse staring at them. They both got out of the car but the mouse remained there while they looked on dumbstruck because on this night, of all nights, they were watching the only mouse that they had ever seen anywhere near the house in all the many years they had lived there.

§ § §

Although Ted was singing amazingly strongly, he and Jackie finally decided, in 1999, that they would not take on any more concert or cabaret work. Their announcement left audiences surprised and disappointed but Ted had always vowed that he would quit while he was winning. "And after all, I am 80," he said.

But reaching four score years did not mean he was retiring entirely. He has a tale to tell and people want to share his experiences. His new world is one of speaking engagements at luncheon clubs, corporate functions and an occasional cruise ship engagement. He reminisces, relates humorous anecdotes about the people he worked with – and, inevitably, and with surprising power, he drops in a few bars of unaccompanied singing and this always goes down well.

A sad loss in what can only ever be regarded as 'semi retirement' was of Stella, who had been on stage everywhere with them since she had been a pup, generating adoring 'aaahs' in the audience. She was nearly 14, and anyone who has loved and lost a dog can imagine the feeling of desolation people they experienced over the passing of an animal that has become part of the team, and part of the family. But once again, after two miserable weeks, they could not resist the temptation; they found Barney, a nine-month-old yellow Labrador who happened to share the same relatives, in his pedigree, with Stella.

Ted says: "He is so handsome, has a beautiful nature and is very affectionate". Jackie adds: "Barney has already made his first public appearance, at one of Ted's speaking engagements where he stole the limelight, with the Press photographers saying 'This way, Barney!" and "Over here Barney!"

"We didn't mind."

As Ted said: "Well, we've had our share of the limelight!'"

Some famous faces in the cast of Aladdin at the Shaftsbury Theatre. The line up included Richard O'Sullivan, Roy Kinnear, Derreck Griffiths, Tommy Trinder and Lindsey de Paul. Right: 'The Emperor' shakes hands with 'the Duke'. Doing the introduction is 'Panto King' Paul Elliott.

Above: 25 years after being approached to appear in The Sound Of Music I appeared as Captain Von Trapp in a provincial production, alongside Isla St Clair.

Right: As Buffalo Bill in Annie Get Your Gun at the Aldwich in London.

CHAPTER 19

"Dad said: 'The boy can sing' but neither thought I'd make a living from it"

Now it's time for Ted to add a postscript in his own words, and add a few thoughts and a few more anecdotes....

As the song goes, *If You Asked Me I Could Write A Book*. Well, you could ask me – but writing a book at my age? Well, I would never have attempted it without my great friend, Neil Patrick, who has been inspirational in every way.

Nearly 15 years ago, Neil, the newly-appointed editor of YOURS, at that time just a monthly newspaper of few pages, rang one day and asked if he could arrange an interview. We hit it off immediately and Jackie and I have watched with admiration the way he developed this fragile paper into a powerful big-selling magazine, full of encouragement for the 'fifties and over' to enjoy their later years to the full. An incredible success.

The task of getting together material for the book seemed insurmountable and it certainly set the 'old and grey' matter in a frenzy just trying to remember that far back, over all those years. My lovely Jackie, who has done so much of the research for me, used to curse my tendency to hoard things, but in this case it paid off.

She managed to find, up in our loft, some old diaries going back as far as Carousel. Although I never kept a day-to-day account, I did include most of my important dates, which has proved to be invaluable. And even now memories keep flooding in. And here are some more of them I would like to share with you...

Going back to my boyhood in beautiful Vancouver, I still remember those early days with great affection. The sudden transformation from a city lad to a country boy at the age of 14 could have been traumatic. I might have hated it ...but no, I fell for it in every way.

I suddenly became conscious of all living creatures; trying to save injured animals; delivering calves at birth; and, at farrowing time, staying up half the night for one of our sows, to dry each baby piglet and pop it into a big box with a warm kerosene lamp, until the entire litter was born, making sure none were frozen or smothered by their mother's bulk.

And now for the first time, I was working with my father. We were a team. There was nothing he couldn't put his hand to, typical of the pioneering folk of his time. But, more than that, he was knowledgeable, had a great sense of fun, and was totally supportive of the young son who came so much later than the first three. "The boy can sing…really sing", he would say to my mother, but neither of them, at that stage, could envisage me ever making living at it. Because of my love of animals, they thought I might follow in the footsteps of one of our distant relatives who had been a vet.

I can honestly say, all four sons adored their dad, but I was the lucky one in that I could work shoulder to shoulder with him for four years on the farm, and reach deep into his character to find so much to admire. Like the time when we went out hunting together and I was walking behind him with my gun. He had always taught me to make sure that the safety catch was safely on.

I stumbled and the gun went off, the bullet landing in the ground just behind my father's feet. I was absolutely mortified in the realisation that I could have killed my beloved dad. All he did was to turn around and give me the hardest stare he could, knowing by my horrified expression that that was all that was needed. I shall never ever forget it! Nor will I forget my darling little mother…so talented musically and artistically. She taught me all the basic music theory that later made it so easy to develop my career as a singer.

§ § §

Now let me share another memory, from wartime days….

On one of my first leaves in London, I recall when, with three pals of mine from our Squadron, we decided to go to a musical one evening. Although the name Ivor Novello meant nothing to four rookies from Canada, we were keen to familiarise ourselves with everything British. Seated in the circle, we couldn't believe the surrounding audience, almost all swooning females, even before the curtain had gone up! What we didn't know then was, that Ivor was their idol, particularly to the slightly older ladies.

In the scene when Ivor was supposed to leap through a window into the bedroom of his beloved (played by Roma Beaumont) he caught his toe and crashed down, winding himself, writhing in pain and momentarily 'holding up the plot.' Roma, in her panic, forgot who she was and stepped out of character and shouted – "Ivor, Ivor, are you all right?" The female audience gasped in horror. But, of course, we thought it was incredibly funny and roared with laughter. We just made it out of the theatre without being lynched!

But back to today. I can never begin to express my emotional thoughts for the girl whose eyes captivated and mesmerised me 53 years ago (and still do!). She hasn't just been my wonderful wife (though we don't know, or care, where the marriage certificate is!) but a wonderful mother to the two great sons she gave me. She has shared a lifetime of music and theatre with me, being the lovely dancer and singer she is; and, through the years, we have been fantastic lovers.

In the earliest days of our romance, Jackie asked me to have lunch with her in the flat she and Terry had rented. She had prepared a meal for the two of us, the first she had attempted for me.

Because she had been on stage professionally from the age of 16, she knew her culinary expertise was limited, and she was nervous. So nervous, in fact, that suddenly there was a loud crash from the kitchen. I did exactly what she hoped I would not do. I rushed in to help, and discovered that she had dropped a bowl of peas all over the floor. However, no prompting was needed. Well, any excuse to mushing around together on a kitchen floor… But, the first time with peas!

And here's a racing memory. Soon after Jackie and I had married we met Harry Carr (the Queen's jockey for many years) and his charming wife Joan. We were invited to join their party for their 25th wedding anniversary at his stud farm in Newmarket, with their son-in-law Joe Mercer and his wife along with Lester Piggott and other top jockeys in attendance. Jackie and I were the odd ones out, but they were interested in showbiz and they made us feel very welcome.

It was a fun evening as the wine flowed, ending up with the top lads of racing, marking our card for winners in all the races over the next two days at Newmarket. Result… a great day at the races, but only one win out of twelve tipped by the jockeys! As they laughingly put it: 'We never know who's going to win. We just ride the damn things, and that's why we only give our wives a couple of quid to bet with!"

When Jackie was nearly five months pregnant with Stephen, we had a two-week break in a villa in Menton, France. Eric Morecambe and Ernie Wise were shooting The Riviera Touch at that time, and we had tentatively made arrangements with them before we left to meet them some time while we were down there, when they had a break from filming. After a couple of days we had a call from Nice, asking us to join them for a meal in a great bistro they knew of.

By the time we arrived, Ernie and Eric and their wives, Doreen and Joan, and other people had joined the party, people who were also filming down there at that time, Lionel Jeffries and his wife, Warren Mitchell, and Hills and Green, the two script writers who helped to make The Morecambe and Wise show such a success.

The bistro was in a cellar, with brilliant décor and atmosphere as well as two 'wandering minstrels' ambling around the tables, singing and strumming their guitars. The wine flowed, and so did the stream of side-splitting stories at our table. Suddenly, Eric burst out with a vocal of their hit record at that time, Boom Ooh Ya Ta Ta Ta!

Next, Ernie and Lionel joined in, and soon we were all at it. The French at the other tables just could not believe what they were hearing, but seemed highly amused at the good natured fun. The two serenaders suddenly disappeared, and we thought we must have offended them, but not a bit of it. They reappeared again with maracas for Eric and Ernie. That was all that was needed. From then on, everything they played finished up with a vocal finale of Boom Ooh Ya Ta Ta Ta. Jackie, who was pregnant at the time, laughed so much that to this day she attributes Stephen's wonderful sense of humour to that crazy night, one we shall never forget.

There are so many laughter-filled memories to recall. When doing the cabaret for a Jewish Society in the Grosvenor Hotel, London, I was winding up my act with *C'est Magnifique* from Can-Can, coaxing individual ladies to do the 'Ooh la la, c'est magnifique' as I sang each line of the lyric. Naturally I looked for the prettiest ones present, and for my final choice, I held the mike to a truly gorgeous creature who vocalised ultra-sexually and leapt up and gave me a kiss. The crowd loved it. But what really sent them roaring was when, slightly taken aback, I blurted out: "Holy Moses!". For one brief second I thought: "That's finished it. I will have offended someone." Then to my relief the room exploded with laughter, and no one laughed harder that a group of rabbis at the head table.

Of course, there have been dramas along the way. In the seventies The New Stanley Hotel in Nairobi, Rhodesia, was booming. The world of casinos had arrived there. Tree Tops was the absolute 'must' for tourists; safaris could be arranged; Kilimanjaro and Mount Kenya were sights to behold. The New Stanley Hotel was a date not to be missed, said my friend, Dickie Henderson. "I've just been there, Ted," he said. "Go for it."

I did just that, taking with me my MD, at that time, Jack Martin. There was immediate drama when after only a quarter of the flight had gone by, it was announced that the water system on the jet had broken down. The plane was packed and many of the passengers were families with children. No drinking water, no tea, no coffee, no washing facilities or flushing toilets. It was a nightmare for everyone, especially for little ones and their mums. Older folk drowned there sorrows in alcohol… and by the time we landed, half the passengers literally fell off the plane.!

The Grill Room had a sensational atmosphere. It was a joy to perform there every night, with audiences from all over the world. The museums, such as the historical Railway Museum were fascinating. Fine buildings were everywhere, especially the New Hilton Hotel with its ultra-American style. To Jack Martin's consternation – he was staying at the Hilton – beautiful African ladies in exquisite western attire were always available in the foyer for a 'chat!' (what a shame I was staying at the New Stanley!).

The management of the hotel, delighted with our show, took us to Tree Tops for a weekend break. There we spent most of our time on the viewing platform, absorbed by the constant parade of animal and bird life all around us and beneath us.

CHAPTER NINETEEN

One amusing moment was when a few dozen elderly and rather dignified British tourists suddenly found a pair of monkeys dropping in among them. It wasn't their presence that made the ladies blush, but the monkey business that happened to be going on!

I have always loved my work and singing has been a great joy to me. There is nothing quite like the feeling of a job well done and the feedback an audience can give an artist after a good performance. The buzz you get is topped with a feeling of tremendous satisfaction that you have made the life of someone else a little happier. The wonderful letters I have received and the great support I have had from my Appreciation Society over the years, have been fantastic and much appreciated. But, I have never been [stage-struck[as such, and can leave it all behind me at the theatre, returning to my family, who have meant so much to me.

Ian and Cliff have both worked hard in their chosen careers and have been successful. Though we don't see them that often, when we do have a family get-together, the four brothers always have a laugh and the feeling is of tremendous warmth. At the time of writing, Cliff is the only one of the boys to marry, and he waited until he was in his forties. He now has a son, Fraser, whom he adores, our 'foster' grandson. The other guys have always had feminine company and whether or not they choose to marry is their business, and does not worry us one bit. Murray and Sue, his partner, who is a great gal, are, at the moment, in their 13th year together. They are not superstitious!

In career terms, as yet, Murray and Stephen have yet to have the break they deserve, and that is not just two very proud parents talking but the opinion of everyone that sees them perform as song-writer/musicians and singers. For song writers it has never been tougher. Once one could live off the royalties of a successful song, but now it can just be downloaded off the internet for virtually nothing. However, they are now making an impression in Europe, so maybe that is where their future lies. Celebrity is not what they crave, but just the chance to enjoy the one life they have, and at the same time, receive some recognition of their talent. They have their priorities right.

When I was 18 the lady who was to become 'Queen Mum' made her first visit to Canada and one of the Mounties assigned for her escort was my brother Ralph. He's the one on the right in the picture above next to King George VI. The picture below shows his kid brother, 30 years later, shaking hands with the Queen Mother at the Palladium.

Left: Jackie and I relax with the great jazz pianist George Shearing and his wife during the 25th anniversary cruise of the QE2 to New York.

Right: Jackie and I doing a duet in the Grand Lounge on the anniversary cruise.

Left: Marion Montgomery (centre) also entertained on the cruise.

Artist Terry Cuneo taught me so much about painting. In this picture we are in the studio of the artist who was a direct descendent of Garibaldi, the Italian statesman.
Right: Cuneo's portrait of Jackie. He called it 'The Lady In the green Gloves'.

Jackie and the boys in Terry's studio in front of one of the train paintings for which he was famous.

Right: Terry joined me in firing up a real steam locomotive on the Nene Valley Railway in Peterborough.

When I reached 70 the Appreciation Society kindly arranged a wonderful surprise for me at the Worthing Pavilion. Joining me on stage was a group made up of family and friends. From the left, in this picture capturing a memorable moment, Ian Hockridge, Terry Cryer, son Murray and Murray my brother, Luanne (Murray senior's daughter), Jackie, Barry Cryer, Elly and Jeffrey Holland. In front are Stephen Hockridge and Cliff, and Stella.

CHAPTER
20

"*There must be someone up there who created this incredible beauty*"

Thinking back on my life, I can't help feeling that I have been a very lucky guy indeed. And I am grateful, so very grateful! When I think about my three older brothers I can't help being affected by the sadness that affected their lives. Jack, the youngest of the three, was kicked in the groin while playing rugby as a young man, and the injury was so bad he was unable to father children, so he and his wife, Margaret, adopted a boy and a girl. The boy, Doug, tragically died in his early twenties of alcoholism.

Later, when Jack and Margaret finally retired after successfully running a construction firm for years, they hoped to have some happy years of playing golf together, a passion they both shared. Sadly, they both died before they could really enjoy what they had worked so hard for over the years.

Ralph, the Mountie (or Brick, as he was known to all his friends) had two children, Wendy and her younger brother, Darrell. Wendy, a great gal and a real character, like her dad, became a nurse and graduated in London, at the end of the Sixties, at the National Heart Hospital. She met Bruce, a young doctor from Newcastle, whom she married. He later became an eminent surgeon, making a very successful career in medicine in Victoria, on Vancouver Island. At that same time, back in Canada, Darrell, who was in this first year at university, met a girl who lured him away to a commune run by one of those weird sects, and the family never saw or heard of him again.

It nearly killed his mother, Alice. Brick, as always, the strong and stoical one, took it on the chin, and he never spoke of it. But, it must have hurt so much deep down, and this later took its toll. When approaching the age of 70, and still a very vigorous and energetic man who had never had a day's illness in his life, he was struck down with a paralysing disease, transverse myelitis. The doctors told him that had he been in his forties he might have had a chance of beating it.

Typically he fought on for several years, and learned to drive a specially-adapted car for a wheelchair, with special controls on the wheel of the car, so that he could remain as independent as possible, being the proud man he was. When I took Jackie and the boys to Canada to see him in 1980, he gave us all a great time, insisting on driving us around

Victoria, Vancouver Island, where he lived. An amazing man – such courage!

My eldest brother, Murray, achieved great success in the British Columbia education system. He lived to the age of 89, but lost his dear wife, Grace, and then saw his youngest daughter, Luanne, lose her fight with cancer in her late fifties. It was a terrible loss not only to him, but to her beloved big sister, Pat, another super gal (the two of them were so close).

Though I was born into a family who were regular churchgoers, I am not religious in that way. My religion is looking at a beautiful flower or living creature, or a magnificent tree and thinking that there must be someone up there who created all this incredible beauty, but I cannot believe that he or she is only interested in one type of religious sect, to the exclusion of all others!

We, as a family, just love the idea of that great James Stewart movie It's A Wonderful Life, and Jackie and I have adopted his guardian angel, called Clarence. We often say: "Thank you, Clarence, for all our good fortune"

§ § §

Now turn the page for a peep into the Hockridge family album

Above: With Jackie at a party in Torquay. We were just married and more in love than ever.

Right: A record company publicity photograph taken in front of our home.

So happy! On our honeymoon trip across Canada in our own private suite on the Canadian Pacific Railway. Three days and four nighs of fantastic food, scenery and service. Pure joy for us having waited nine years.

**Above: Visiting
Ian at Seaford
College.**

**Right: One of
my favourite
pictures...
Jackie with
Murray.**

In showbusiness it's great to have fans making you the centre of attention!

There's something fishy about this one (a bass not a baritone!)

Harry Carr (the Queen's jockey for almost 20 years) with his wife Joan and Jackie the morning after their 25th wedding anniversary.

The great Peter Knight, conductor and arranger supremo. He was responsible for many of my 250 recordings over the years.

Jackie and I on holiday in Egypt.

Left: Jackie cutting Roy Castles hair in the garden of our rented house in Blackpool. We were appearing at different theatres but we would get together when we could. Roy started out as a barber and gave Jackie a lesson in hair cutting and ended up being the guinea pig!

Below: Three crazy caballeros on the Bruce forsyth show. Roy Castle(right) with Bruce Forsyth (centre) and myself

Keeping it in the family. Stephen (14) on bass guitar and Murray (16) on drums joined me on stage as part of my backing group. It was a two hour concert and they were both sensational.

The Hockridge family show. Left to right: Stephen, Edmund, Jackie and Murray

An unexpected reunion with Roy Castle and Dennis King.

Above: Even Stella likes YOURS magazine.

Left: Barney Hockridge – our fourth labrador over the years.

Jackie and I with Harry Secombe when he came to our home town to film his TV show Highway.

With Barbara Windsor - we appeared together in Ian Liston's excellent Hiss & Boo Music Hall shows.

HEY THERE

Thank you
Neil Patrick would like to thank the following for their help in producing Hey There: Linda (his wife), and Trina Bache for checking the manuscript; Michael Oke and Mary Ann Fulcher for their valued opinions; Sharon Reid for design magic and Lauren Patrick for help with inputting. It goes without saying that without the enormous contribution of the 'Hockridge Clan', the book could not have been written!

Design by Sharon Reid (contact: sharon.reid57@ntlworld.com)